CW00919257

HOW TO GET STARTED IN GOLF

How to get started in golf

with illustrations by Alex Hay

Henry Longhurst

CORONET BOOKS
Hodder Paperbacks Ltd., London

Printed and bound in Great Britain for
Coronet Books,
Hodder Paperbacks Ltd,
St. Paul's House, Warwick Lane,
London, EC4P 4AH
by Hazell Watson & Viney Ltd,
Aylesbury, Bucks

ISBN 0 340 02439 9

Contents

i. Welcome to golf

FOR more years than I should care to admit I have been playing, watching, writing and broadcasting about golf, but in all
this time I have rarely encouraged anyone to take it up. I have
never tried to "sell" golf and am not trying to do so now.
Golf, in one's life, is what used at school to be termed a
"voluntary subject". You don't have to take it unless you elect
to do so. So if I mention now some of the attractions that
make it unique among games, it is because the very fact that
you have this book in your hand means that you have already
felt some interest in it.

People, as you know, get "bitten" by golf—sometimes to an

7

almost ludicrous extent. I myself, as I have recounted elsewhere, was "bitten" at the age of eleven. This, I thought, is
the game for me, and so it has proved for the rest of my life.

Looking back, I think its main advantages, out of many, are
two. The first is that it is almost the only outdoor game that
for the whole of your active life, from eight to eighty, you can
actually *play*. You can, of course, watch it as well, but you
do not, as cricketers and footballers do, get relegated to the
sidelines as you grow older. Golf is the supreme "do it yourself" game. Nobody is trying to bowl you out, or kick you on
the shins, or snatch the ball from you. Everyone stands still
and silent while you play your shot. If it is a failure, you have
only yourself to blame—though you will be surprised what
other outside influences some golfers do find to blame! On
the other hand, if it is a success, well, alone you did it and
yours is the glory.

The second, and in this case absolutely unique, advantage
of golf is that it is the only game in which the good and the
bad player can play together to the equal satisfaction of both.
You simply cannot, with real pleasure to all, play out of your
class—either above or below it—in tennis, football, squash,
cricket, or even snooker. In golf you have your handicap, of
which I shall say something later, and, if you keep your head
and don't get frightened, there is no reason why, aided by this
handicap, you should not beat Arnold Palmer. What is perhaps
more important, there is no reason why Palmer should not
thoroughly enjoy playing with you.

There are, of course, other advantages. One is that whereas
most outdoor games, and many indoor, are played on a standard kind of pitch, or court, there are more than 1,500 golf
"pitches" in Britain alone and not only is every one of them
different from the others, but each consists of 18 little
"pitches", or holes (in some cases 9), which are themselves

different from all the others. This, incidentally, is only one of the reasons which make golf such an ideal game for your annual holiday.

Golf, again, is now played all over the civilised world—and, in my own experience, in a good deal of the "uncivilised" world too. Wherever you go, if you are lucky enough to travel, you will find a golf club, nearly always happy to welcome the visiting stranger. If you are a business man visiting a distant country, never mind the letters of introduction. Get into the golf club. Golf is the Esperanto of sport. The man who misses a four-foot putt in Tokyo experiences precisely the same feelings as the man who does it in Timbuktoo.

Finally, golf, if you are lucky, can take you to some of the most lovely scenery in the world. At home our little island is the golfing treasure house of the world. We play on heath and meadow; in ancestral parks and on the moors; high up on the Downs; and, what no other country possesses and we think to be the greatest golf of all, on the "linksland"—hence the term golf "links"—the rolling sand dunes which remained as the link between land and sea when the sea receded millions of years ago.

One final quality does, I like to think, make golf unique. You really cannot play tennis on the Centre Court at Wimbledon, or cricket at Lord's, or football at Wembley—but you can, and should, play on the great championship links where golfing history has been made. The problems which the champions faced on great occasions in the past are the problems that you are facing now. Sometimes they will have driven from tees a little farther back, but that is all.

Perhaps the most famous golf hole in the world is the 17th, or Road Hole, on the Old course at St. Andrews. Here, eating into the green, is a deep little sand bunker, only a few paces across either way. As you stand in it, wondering how you can

9

get the ball up and out and yet stop it before it rolls over the green and into the road (from which you may well knock it back into the bunker), you may reflect that you are standing within a few feet of where pretty well every great golfer in the game's history has at some time stood, looking at precisely the same scene, thinking precisely the same thoughts—"Must get out. Mustn't go over. Why did I get in?"

And, as you proceed to the last hole, you may reflect that in the open championship of 1964 Jack Nicklaus, with a gale behind, drove on to the green—382 yards—in all four rounds, and in the play off against Doug Sanders in 1970 actually drove through the green. Or you may remember seeing on the television both Bobby Locke and Kel Nagle, winners in 1957 and 1960, pitching their final shots to within three feet of the hole. You are standing this time on precisely the same tee as they did. Maybe the hole does not look so simple now as it did on the television—but the fact remains that you personally, in your humble way, are privileged to play on exactly the same ground on which the game's history was made.

So, welcome to golf, the game of a lifetime. One very old friend of mine, a past Walker Cup Captain, was a highly proficient player at the age of six. Only last year I played two rounds in one day with a veteran player who, I thought, tired a little towards the end. No wonder. It turned out that he was 83. When I look back at all the fun and the friendships it has given me, in so many parts of the world, I only wish I could be starting all over again!

ii. What *is* golf?

THE game of golf, if I may write for a moment for the completely uninitiated, is essentially a business of starting here and finishing there, overcoming as best you may all the hazards encountered on the way and endeavouring to get your ball into the hole in fewer strokes than the other man. You start on a flat teeing-ground, generally known simply as the tee, and for your opening stroke at each hole you may tee the ball up on a wooden or plastic peg (or anything else you fancy: a very well known plastic surgeon used sometimes to drive the ball off the top of a beer bottle) and this peg is also known as a tee. For all other shots, apart from exceptions noted later under "The

Rules", the sacred rule of golf is that you must play the ball as it lies and must do nothing whatever to improve its lie. In a sand bunker you may not even ground your club behind it, because obviously the weight of the club alone would make a "dent" in the sand sufficient to improve the lie of the ball.

You hope that your drive from the tee will finish on the broad expanse of cut grass known as the fairway. This is bordered on either side by the rough, which may consist of thick grass, bracken, heather, bushes, woods and what not, and may be bounded by an out-of-bounds in the shape of anything from a railway line to a plain wire fence. There are also on many courses a variety of water hazards and the number of balls retrieved from them every year is phenomenal.

Eventually you arrive at the green, a specially prepared expanse of lawn—in some cases of really fantastic excellence—on which you try to putt the ball into a 4¼-inch hole—putt rhyming with "but" in the South of England and with "soot" in the North.

As you play from the fairway, you will probably hack out a lump of turf, known as a divot, and it is one of the first points of golfing etiquette to replace and stamp down these divots. On some courses, however—St. Andrews in particular comes to mind—the crows come and peck the divots out the moment your back is turned, but it is still good form to put them back. Likewise, in a bunker you try to straighten out the footmarks you have left in the sand. It is annoying enough to get into a bunker at all, without landing in somebody else's heel mark as well.

Courses consist—I honestly don't know why—of 18 holes, or in some cases 9, and this applies all over the world. They range from something around 6,000 yards, which is reckoned short, to the 7,100 yards to which most courses are stretched for the open championship. An average course would have perhaps four short holes, reachable in one shot from the tee by a medium-good player, anything from 140–250 yards; four long holes, more than 475 yards long, which he cannot normally reach in two shots; and the rest, ranging from 250–475 yards, which he is able, more easily or less, to reach in two.

Clubs these days have lost their original individual names, except the driver and the putter, and are now known—and the more's the pity—merely by numbers. Starting with the driver as No. 1, there are five wooden clubs, each with a little bigger angle of loft on the face of the club, and a little less length of shaft, than the one before. If hit fairly and squarely, I dare say the ball would go 10–15 yards less far with each club, the longest being the No. 1 and the shortest the No. 5. Nobody, of course, carries all five, though more of that later, and similarly nobody—or very few—carry all the irons, which range straightforwardly from Nos. 1 to 10, each one, as the number increases, calculated to hit the ball less far, but more sharply upwards. Beyond the No. 10, or in some sets the No. 9, there are a variety of clubs known generally as wedges and one of these, which I have described under "Equipment", may soon become of use to the beginner.

Whenever you set out to play golf, you have three opponents —yourself, the course and the other man. You might even add a fourth—the game of golf itself. Indeed, to the newcomer this will at first be the stiffest opponent of the four.

As to learning to make golf shots, I can only compare it with learning to play the piano. You are asking a whole series of muscles to perform actions to which they are unaccustomed and in each case there is no substitute for "playing scales". The only encouragement I can give, having experienced both, is to say that "playing scales" at golf is liable to be a great deal more fun than playing them on the piano.

In other words, the only way to learn to play golf is to go on hitting golf shots. This is not an instructional book but I will give one piece of instruction—namely, "Do get some instruction"! You will find, as with most things in this life, that you do not at first succeed in doing what you are trying to do. Of course not, but it will save heaven knows how much time, energy and frustration if what you are trying to do is correct. Then, as you gradually improve, at least you are getting nearer to achieving what is right rather than getting better at being bad, if you see what I mean.

I am not referring to complicated instruction, like "Where should the left shoulder point at the top of the swing?", of which, heaven knows, you are liable to get enough later on. I mean simply that trial and error over the best part of a century has shown that, within reasonable limits, there is a right way to hold the club, a right way to stand, a right place to have the ball in relation to your feet, and so on. Any professional or good amateur could tell you in ten minutes what it might take you years of discouragement to find out for yourself—if indeed you ever did. Take his word for it and save the time. If you cannot find the necessary expert—and even if you can—I would refer you to the, as I think, quite exceptionally intelligible instruction by Peter Thomson, five times British Open champion, in Chapter XI.

Apart from the business of learning to hit the ball, your next most serious opponent, assuming that you become "bitten" with the game, is likely to be yourself. It is quite astonishing how infuriating this simple game can be—which, of course, is part of its charm. Perhaps the main reason is that you have no one else to blame. When bowled out in cricket, you can return to the pavilion declaring that "that ball would have bowled Bradman". In golf nobody tries to hinder you. It's all yours. You declare your intention of hitting the ball 100 yards in a given direction on to a large expanse of green. The world stands back in silence—and you hit it practically at right angles, knee-high, into a pond. In my younger days the game used to drive me into frenzies of rage. If you find the same, well, we are in good company, since the world's greatest golfer, Bobby Jones, was in his early days nearly driven mad by it, too. I know no aspect of life in which you can be so much "your own worst enemy" as in golf. The essence of it is to forget the bad shot and get on with the next one. Easier said than done!

All this is why practically no one ever gives up golf. If you are playing well, why rob yourself of this exquisite satisfaction? If you couldn't hit your hat, you'll be hanged if you will be defeated by a game that only consists of hitting a little ball along with a little stick!

iii. What do you need? how much should it cost?

Clubs

I have already referred to the various types of club, their names, numbers, and what they do—or are meant to do. We now come to the question of how many do you need, and what ought they to cost you. Before I answer, let me put you into the background picture.

Till the early thirties a player's "set" of golf clubs was simply those clubs which he chose to carry. They tended to cost £1 or so apiece—7s. 6d. before the First War—and they had hickory shafts. These varied greatly in quality and it was fun to watch the professional picking them out from the great bundle in his shop, bending and twisting them and appraising the straightness of the grain in order to pick out the best for the new driver that he was going to make for you. When you visited another club, you instinctively made for the pro's shop and waggled some of the many clubs on show. The bore the old-fashioned names—driver, brassie, and spoon—or baffy —for the woods: driving-iron, mid-iron, mashie, mashie-niblick and niblick, plus many other "extras" like cleek, jigger, and so forth, for the irons. If a club took your fancy, you added it to your set.

As the game grew more popular, especially across the length and breadth of the United States, the supply of good hickory, and of persimmon for the wooden club heads, began to run out. and steel shafts were the inevitable outcome. They were easier to make, easier to play with (a bad shot is not nearly so bad with steel as it would have been with hickory) and, above all, they made it possible to "match" clubs, one to the other, so that they all swung alike. It was steel shafts that gave rise to the "grooved swing" so long coveted among golfers, though not so fashionable perhaps today.

Whereas a good player's set of clubs in the hickory days would be anything from, say, eight to eleven—Harry Vardon won the last of his five open championships with eight—when steel arrived, a number of bright spirits began adding more and more clubs to their armoury, until you had the ridiculous spectacle of young fellows playing in the amateur championship with as many as 22, contained in a vast bag which the luckless caddie could hardly lift to his shoulder. The fact that the great Walter Hagen was paid 500 dollars a year for every club of a certain make which he carried round in his bag, and at one time had 25, may have had something to do with it!

At any rate the authorities stepped in on both sides of the Atlantic and decided that a limit must be placed on the number of clubs and that this limit should be 14. No one, I am sure, foresaw what would result and what an influence it would have on the game. What happened was that instead of a man's "set" being simply the number he chose to carry—adding one here, discarding one there—almost overnight a "set of clubs" became 14. The maximum became the minimum.

You most emphatically do *not* need the maximum to begin with—though I expect you will get round to it in the end. You will need at first at least one wooden club, preferably two. The first you will use to drive with, though it should not, I think, be a driver. Since you will use it from at least 14 tees in 18 holes, and possibly on the fairway too, it is an important club and worth taking trouble over. I recommend what used to be called a brassie and is now more likely to be unromantically known as a 2- or 3-wood. This will have more loft than a driver, and will make it easier to get the ball into the air (see the hint on "Hitting it forwards" on page 75, which might save you weeks of difficulty in getting the ball up).

Most people, though not all, find it easier to hit the ball from the fairway, or from a good lie in the rough, with a lofted wooden club than with one of the bigger irons. You will soon detect which category you belong to. If, like me, you are a wooden club man, then I recommend most strongly that your second club should be a 5-wood—the maid of all work or, as I like to think of it, the "poor man's friend". This is the most lofted of all standard wooden clubs and the easiest to play. If on the other hand you find iron clubs easier, get a 3-iron instead of the 5-wood. When hit properly, the ball will go about the same distance with each, so you certainly don't need both.

If you have a 5-wood, get a 4-iron and a 6 and an 8. If a 3-iron, then go on with irons 5, 7 and 9.

You have now got an ample equipment of 5 clubs, and a

putter makes six. So far as I can see, absolutely any putter will do. Some prefer a solid aluminium-headed affair, others prefer the simple "blade" variety, which is no more than a shortened iron club with no loft at all. You may pick one up cheap in a lost property office and use it all your life, or you may, as many do, finish up with an umbrella-stand full of the damned things.

Sooner or later you will come round to getting what is now generally known as a "wedge". If your set otherwise ends with the 8-iron, then get the wedge sooner rather than later. If you have a 9-iron, there is less hurry. The wedge will be the most lofted club in your bag and it *must* pass one acid test. Hold it up by the bottom of the shaft, at eye-level and with the head pointing towards you. The rear edge of the sole (those who remember their wartime aircraft recognition will know it as the trailing edge) must be lower than the leading edge. This means that when pitching from grass or excavating the ball from bunkers, you can get the feeling of thumping the back of the sole on to the ground or into the sand rather than cutting into it with the front edge. The old-fashioned niblick nearly always had a sharp front edge and was the very devil to play with. At the slightest lifting of your head or relaxing your grip, this sharp edge would bite into the ground and the shot would be ruined.

The original club built on the rear-edge-lower principle was popularised by Gene Sarazen, who put a lining of lead on the back of a standard niblick and came over from the United States with it to win the British Open in 1932. He called it a sand-iron. Tommy Armour, another winner of the Open on both sides of the Atlantic, regards it as the greatest single factor in the lower scores of today as against those in the 20's. So does Sam Snead. It is still by no means a standardised club but, when you have played for a while with your first clubs and begin to get the feel of things, you will appreciate what I mean about wedges in general. When you come across one that feels right and corresponds to your other clubs in weight (don't, whatever you do, be foisted off with some extra-heavy kind of "bludgeon"), I recommend it as the first addition to your set.

Just as you do not need a vast number of clubs to begin with, so you do not in my opinion need new ones. The luxury of new clubs comes later and will give you a thrill equal almost to your first bicycle.

Where do you find used clubs? Once again—a constant theme in this book—our old friend, the club professional. Any professional: any club. Used clubs should be obtainable at anything from a maximum of forty shillings apiece, for very good specimens, downwards. Or maybe you know a family where someone has given up golf—a very rare type, I may add!—or, sad to say, has died, in which case there may be a perfectly good set of clubs going begging in the attic.

Nor at first need you worry about what kind of shafts your clubs have. This too comes later. Steel shafts are a work of astonishing precision and vary in their degree of flex or "whip". To get the best out of the stiffest shafts, you need to be not only a good player but a very strong one. As the game begins to get under your skin and you contemplate venturing on new clubs, take advice, again from the professional, and ask him what are the shafts best suited to your ability, strength and sex.

Having decided upon this, say no more at the moment but spend some time, possibly months, looking at sets of clubs in professionals' shops, in sporting stores and, of course, in other people's bags. Eventually, after many flirtations, you will fall in love and will know that this time it is the "real thing". When you appreciate that there are three different qualities of shaft and that the top quality alone is made in 14 different lengths—four for woods, nine for irons, and one for the putter, and all with varying degrees of flexibility—and furthermore that there are innumerable different types of clubhead, you will appreciate that the number of combinations and permutations approaches the football pool level. No professional, nor even a big store, can stock them all, but all are readily available and can be ordered for you as easily as a bookseller can order a book.

Buying a new set of golf clubs is an expensive landmark in the life of the average golfer. When the time comes, which may not be for a year or two after you first pick up this book, wait till you have seen a set that really thrills you, then order them duly married to the shafts that will give you the most help.

Trolleys and Bags

In golf's earliest days the players used only a few clubs—some with delightfully descriptive names like the "rut-iron", for getting out of cart tracks—and these few were carried round under the arm, sometimes by the player himself but more generally by a rather scruffy-looking boy or occasionally by a more senior character known often, I regret to say, for his general partisanship and an obvious failure to have signed the pledge. Gradually, it may have been in the 70's and 80's, it seemed more sensible to have some sort of container for the clubs, hence the first tube-like bags, of canvas or leather, costing anything from 3s. 6d. upwards. As the game became more sophisticated and golfers began to travel farther afield, pockets were added to the bags, first for balls, then for waterproof clothing. Then came hoods to protect the clubs in transit, followed by bigger and bigger bags to carry more and more clubs

(The present position may entertain, though it will not concern, the newcomer to golf. A "set" of 14 clubs weighs a maximum of about 13 lbs. Jack Nicklaus' bag, complete, weighs 70 lbs., or substantially more than the "full marching order" regarded as the maximum for a soldier of World War I. An American manufacturer has advertised a bag in Britain for 69 guineas and in America itself it is common to have another huge bag in which to carry the bag with the clubs in!)

The question of caddies need not concern us here and the golfer's choice resolves itself into the simple question: Do you carry your clubs round in a bag or do you wheel them round on a trolley? I myself am prejudiced in this matter and admit to being in a minority. I prefer to carry a few clubs round in what has come to be known as a "drainpipe" bag. This has a pair of retractable legs, which keep it up at an angle when you lay it down, and a stiffened sling which remains upright so that you have only to reach your hand down about six inches to pick it up and sling it over your shoulder. The bag will hold about ten clubs but I personally carry eight. If you carry more than this, you will need a bigger and heavier bag and then, it seems to me, a trolley becomes essential.

The advantage of a trolley is that, within reason, weight does not really matter and you can pile on an umbrella, spare woollies, and all the unaccountable paraphernalia that a golfer manages to accumulate, and not really notice the difference. The main disadvantage is that if your ball is, say, to the left of the green and the next tee is away to the right (as it always seems to be!) you have got either to leave your trolley over on the left and then, since you may not take it on the green, go back and get it and wheel it all round the green when you have finished putting, or leave it on the right of the green in the first place and then walk all across the green, carrying a pitching club (which may not be the one you want, anyway) and a putter, in order to get to your ball. Neutral observers, of which

I am not one, reckon that four people pulling trolleys will take from twenty minutes to half an hour longer than the same four carrying their own clubs.

To sum up, I would suggest that in the first instance you obtain the "short" set of clubs I have mentioned—say half-a-dozen—and a small second-hand canvas bag for a few shillings. Then, when you have carried them for a while, hire a trolley for a round or two—for about 30p—and judge for yourself. If you decide to become a "trolleyman", then buy one of your own, for about six or seven pounds, but once again have a good look at other people's first. Some trolleys come along behind you so lightly that you hardly know they are there. Others are heavy, obstinate as mules, and always tipping over on their sides. You should also make sure that your trolley is simple to dismantle and fits easily into the boot of your car.

Clothing

It was the fashion at the turn of the century for the gentleman golfer, especially in Scotland, to turn out in his oldest and most dilapidated clothes. To appear smartly dressed on the links branded a man automatically as a bounder. Gradually the custom changed and "natty" dressing became, between the wars, the hallmark of the golfer. Now we have reverted to something between the two and any sort of reasonably sober attire will do. There are those who, like myself, have an increasing prejudice against the wearing of white caps—perhaps because they are nearly always dirty, and show it—and an even more unreasoning hostility to the sensible practice of tucking the bottom of the trousers into the socks in wet weather, but we may be disregarded as ancient "squares" and, in the language of the day, no longer "with it". One thing you will *not* do, however, is to play golf with no coat—and braces!

What you *must* have for golf, and it may well be in your wardrobe already, is something which will keep you warm enough and at the same time allow you to swing your arms with freedom. You will soon, I fancy, reckon a pair of waterproof trousers to be worthwhile and possibly the jacket as well. Nylon is the obvious choice from the weight point of view but it used to have one great disadvantage. It rustled. The noise as you made a four-foot putt was positively deafening. Now at last you can get a new form of "noiseless nylon", with the coat weighing 10 ounces and the trousers 6. Any professional can get this through his Co-operative Association.

Elsewhere in this book I have mentioned that the two most important fingers in golf are, strangely, the last two on the left hand. It is the left hand that "gives", against the natural striking force of the right. You will not have been playing long, I suspect, before you see the wisdom of buying—from any pro's shop—a left-hand glove. The feeling of extra strength is quite remarkable.

As to shoes, well, you *must* be anchored to the ground. At first you will be "all over the place" anyway, which is bad enough in itself without your feet slipping from under you as well. Walking shoes with ribbed rubber soles are admirable for golf—though rubber soled "sneakers" are not, since they do not support your ankles—but in the end you will come round to a pair of good guaranteed-waterproof golf shoes, with spikes which can be unscrewed and replaced when they wear out. The shoes may cost you a fiver or more but, if you look after them, they will last you for years. There are also some admirably cheap all-rubber shoes complete with spikes.

The Golf Ball

There are two sizes of ball, usually known as the small, or British, ball and the large, or American. In Britain you may play with either; in the United States only with the American. In international matches you may play with either, but this will not, I fancy, concern readers of this book for a while yet. Both types of ball must weigh not less than 1·62 oz. In diameter the British must be not less than 1·62 inches; the American not less than 1·68. The difference in size is only six-hundredths of an inch but to the eye it looks astonishing. Much controversy has raged around these two balls but I shall not muddle the issue here. You will almost certainly start with the small ball and I will say only that, if later on you get a chance of playing a round or two with the other, I should certainly do so.

The best new balls cost around 30p and since you may lose one in a blackberry bush with your very first stroke it would be a ridiculous extravagance to use the best balls, or indeed to use new balls at all. It is very likely that the professional will have a stock of "pick-ups" at around 15p and I can assure you that, if, as a beginner, you stood in one spot and hit two dozen of these and two dozen new balls, they would be all mixed up together with no difference in performance between the two. When you become a member of a club, I might add, it is not "done" to buy balls from anyone except the professional and especially not done to buy them from questionable characters wandering about in the rough and offering them for sale on the course. Later, of course, you will fall for the delicious thrill of extracting a new ball from its paper and plastic cover but I do assure you that it is a waste of money at first.

iv. The beginner's best friend

WHEN you decide at last to take the plunge, how in fact are you going to get started? If you have a friend to set you on your way, well and good. If not, it is a case of either a driving range or a visit to the nearest club professional. Driving ranges have long been a feature of the roadside scene in the United States but only came into their own in England in the early 1960's, coinciding with the same sudden golfing "explosion" which seemed to justify the production of this book. A television programme seen by millions showed a three-tiered floodlit driving range in Japan with balls by the hundred showering out into the darkness, and this added impetus to a movement which at the moment of writing is just beginning to get into its stride. Two ranges at Finchley and Croydon pioneered the way and now a whole network of ranges is planned by Athlon Limited, a company directed by a great teacher and international player, John Jacobs.

If you are lucky enough to live within reach of one of these "golf centres", this is the place to go. Ninety per cent of the other people there will be beginners too. You can hire a club and a bucket of balls—30p for 60 is an average charge—and you then retire to one of a number of "bays", all in a row, and bash away to your heart's content. Nearly all ranges are flood-lit, so you can do it in the evenings—and a very entertaining evening it can make, especially if you go with one or two friends.

And now I come to what is perhaps the most important single sentence in this book. *Do, I beg you, invest in one or two preliminary lessons.* At every club or range you will find a professional or assistant professional who will help to set you on your way, probably at no more than 60p per half hour, and, if ever money proves to have been well spent in your golfing lifetime, this will be it. While there is no "correct" way of swinging a golf club, certain basic fundamentals have become common ground and these may be "taken as read" rather than become the subject of personal trial and error—mainly error—lasting perhaps for years. What has been proved to be the best way of swinging a club, allowing for individual variations, is not on the whole a "natural" movement. A good county cricketer on taking to golf might come quite near to it but the average person rarely does, nor indeed do children, who may well show natural ability in other directions.

Children in fact almost invariably grasp the club with the left hand below the right. Nor is this so unnatural as it may sound, for if you stand with the ball opposite your left foot, which is where it should be for the longer shots, and extend a club towards it, you will find that your left arm is "longer" than your right. The child's instinct tells him to put the hand of the longer arm below that of the shorter. In this connection it may interest the reader to know that an Indian professional, resident in South Africa, called Sewsunker Sewgolum, plays with his left hand below his right and has twice won the Dutch open championship against the best players in Europe.

There are variations in the accepted way of gripping a golf club as well as in swinging it but few people seem to catch hold of the club in the right way at the first time of asking. I think I can help here with a very simple piece of advice. Swing the club with your left arm alone, making sure that you carry it right through along the intended line of flight, and, when the movement begins to feel right, note exactly how you are gripping the club with your left hand. Then repeat the process with the right arm alone. Then start again with both hands, placing them on the club together exactly as you did by themselves. I think you will find that, on looking down, you can see two knuckles of your left hand and that the "V" between your right thumb and forefinger is pointing to your right shoulder. Your hands are now related to the clubhead exactly as were those of Harry Vardon, perhaps the greatest stylist of all time, and this will do to be going on with. Later you may also copy him in moving up the little finger of your right hand to nest in the groove between the first and second fingers of your left, but it will feel very awkward at first and I certainly should not worry about it yet.

Apart from these comments on how to grip the club, I will not anticipate what the professional will tell you about where to stand in relation to the ball, how to get the swing started and such like. I am, however, among those who think that you can learn a lot from books—some, though heaven knows not all—provided they are not too technical or complicated.

My main point here is to emphasise how well worth while it is to take a few preliminary lessons and this brings me to a figure without counterpart, so far as I can see, in other games, namely the professional.

Professionals nowadays fall into two categories, the club pro and the professional player of golf. The great millionaire golfers like Palmer, Nicklaus and Player come in the latter class and, though we may perhaps learn something from watching them, they do not really concern us here. What we are concerned with is what I may without disrespect term the "ordinary club professional". Almost every club in the land has its resident professional, but he may also be found both at driving ranges and at some of the bigger sports stores. Wherever he may be, he is the beginner's best friend.

Let me explain his background and his present position. In the earliest days he was a rough and ready fellow, starting probably as a caddie boy and graduating to club-making (the great James Braid, five times open champion, was a club-maker at the Army and Navy Stores) and then to picking up a few shillings for playing round with the "gentlemen". Even up to the 1920's, when I myself started as a boy, it was not customary for the club professional to enter the clubhouse, though of course his status had by then greatly risen, and even at championships the paid contestants did not expect to use the members' clubhouse. This was not considered snobbish at the time, any more than it is considered snobbish that caddies are not permitted in the clubhouse today.

As time went on, professionals with long service tended to be made honorary members and nowadays in most clubs they are welcome, when they wish, to use the clubhouse. For most of the time, however, if they are not out teaching or playing, they are to be found in their shop adjacent to the clubhouse, which is where they make their living. You do not have to be a member of the club in order to go and talk to the professional or to have lessons with him, nor do you have to pay a green fee. Make a date to go and have a chat with him, and I will bet my bottom dollar that you will find him courteous, considerate and, far from being anxious to take advantage of your inexperience, more likely to start you on your way with less profit than he deserves. From which you will gather that, having numbered them among my friends all my life, I think rather highly of golf professionals.

One thing I would add. A club professional is retained by a club often for only a few pounds a week. Out of this he is expected to keep an assistant, so that the shop may be open when the first member arrives in the morning and close only when the last has left in the evening. He is also expected to keep a good stock of clubs, balls, shoes, sweaters and the like. How then is he to make a living? The answer is through an Unwritten Contract—between him and the golfers who use the club: he to run the shop, they to patronise it. If, as a beginner, you receive a helpful welcome from the pro, as I am sure you will do, it would be nice if you remembered this when, later on, you indulge yourself in an expensive set of new clubs.

v. Starting young

MANY people take to golf only in their forties or fifties and turn into perfectly good players, especially if they have played cricket or tennis or squash and have a natural eye for a ball. All the same there is nothing like starting young—if only for the sake of the extra years during which you are going to get such fun out of the game. For myself, I was eleven. I had never, so far as I can remember, been "aware" of golf, though I suppose I must have known that my father played. We were staying for the family holiday at a hotel overlooking the Common at Yelverton, in Devonshire, and I fell in with a couple of other boys who had cut three holes, probably with a penknife, and used to go out and play before breakfast. This was golf in its crudest original form—no fairways, no greens—just a question of starting here and finishing there and the one that takes the fewest strokes is the winner. It is good, I think, to have started in this way, for it makes you appreciate the true *essence* of golf and realise that the true pleasure comes from the game itself and not from vast clubhouses, swimming pools and four-course lunches, enjoyable as these all may be. Now, more than forty years later, I still prefer clubs with a simple unpretentious clubhouse.

At any rate I went to my father at Yelverton and acquired from him a mashie (about a No. 6 iron in modern terms) and a putter and I believe a third club as well, and, having had the shafts cut down, I joined my two friends on the Common. I was "bitten" by golf, instantly and forever, and it has been part of my life ever since. In the twenties, however, and almost until the war, golf for the young was much frowned upon, especially by schoolmasters, who, though enthusiastic players themselves (golf has always been a schoolmasters' game, I don't know why) took the view that, not being a team game, it did not encourage the "team spirit". The fact that it encouraged complete self-reliance, keep-trying-to-the-end, and many other undoubted virtues, was overlooked, as also was the fact that you cannot be playing cricket *all* the time and that, when you are, you may well be bored to tears. I thought this anti-golf attitude in schools to be wrong at the time and now, looking back, I am sure it was.

Golf is indeed an "old man's game". The beauty of it is, however, that it is also a young man's game, and a young woman's game too. I will go farther. For young men who want to get on in the world I would make it a compulsory subject! When older people say "Do you play golf?", you should be

in a position to say "Yes", even if you add "but not very well".
This means you are "in". Anywhere in the world entré to the
local golf or country club is worth more than a dozen letters
of introduction. Golf opens all the doors.

In my own day as a beginner, living in rural Bedfordshire
where the idea of getting a pitch and twenty-one other boys
in order to play cricket or football would have occurred to no
one, I used to bicycle to the club almost every day and two
or three times a week had a half-hour lesson with the professional, first with the late Jack Seager and then with W. J.
Moore, who retired after 43 years with the club, both of whom
became lifelong friends. These lessons were the highlights of
the week. Life for the youthful enthusiast, however, was no
bed of roses. As a junior, one was not allowed in the clubhouse
and was constantly liable to be ticked off, or at the best glared
at, by retired Indian Army colonels with very white mous-
taches and very red faces.

How different, my dear young fellow, is your lot today! I
well remember, during the "austerity" period after the war,
when it was by no means certain that golf was going to make
any real come-back at all, attending a meeting of interested
parties to see if something could not be done to bring people
into the game, especially the young, practically none of whom
had been able to start golf during the war. This meeting led to
the birth of the Golf Foundation. Not a single person present
can have had any idea of the astonishing success that lay ahead
of it.

The first thing to do, clearly, was to get at young people at
the source, in other words in the schools. At first most head-
masters were far from forthcoming. "No time", or "not a team
game", was the usual story—but gradually progress was made
and the word began to get round that boys and girls at school
were joining the golf classes in ever-increasing numbers. One of

the Golf Foundation's principal allies has been, naturally enough, the Professional Golfers' Association, whose members want to see as many future customers as possible. The enthusiasm with which professionals have entered into coaching schemes in their local schools, often at very low rates, cannot, however, be put down simply to a desire later to sell their pupils some clubs and balls. Ask anyone who has attended these classes or anyone who, like myself, has known golf professionals all his life. Many of them, I really believe, would have done the coaching for nothing. At any rate any junior coming into golf through the Foundation's teaching scheme should lift his hat to the professionals.

From its hesitant start the Foundation at the moment of writing (1967) are giving lessons to no fewer than 26,000 boys and girls in 1,900 schools, colleges, and universities. The Foundation gets its income from various sources (and can always do with more) like subscriptions from the golf trade; a national "week" run by the professionals themselves; and the proceeds of special competitions run by clubs and of the annual Golf Ball at Grosvenor House, London, which is run by the Foundation itself.

So for juniors these days it does seem that the best way of getting into golf, and certainly the easiest and cheapest, is through a school coaching scheme inspired by the Golf Foundation and, if there isn't one at your school, get on the right side of the authorities and see that your school joins the 200 on the waiting list. In the meantime a group of you might "touch" your fathers—who are fathers for, anyway?—and club together to pay the local club professional to come over for an hour every week and get you started on the right lines.

vi. Joining a club

YOU can, of course, play golf without joining a club at all—if you happen to live near enough to a public course and are possessed of very considerable patience. In England public courses are lamentably few and you are liable to have to get up at crack of dawn in order to book a starting time and then have to wait several hours before your turn comes. With the changing climate of opinion towards golf, this position should change in the next ten or fifteen years, but that is of no concern to us today. In Scotland, the "home of golf", public courses are far more numerous, often hard beside the town boundary and on a bus route. It may surprise the beginner to know that, of all places, St. Andrews is a public course. There are, in fact, four St. Andrews courses—the Old, the New, the Eden and the Jubilee—though it is to play on the Old course that pilgrims flock from all over the world. Anyone can play on it for, at the moment, 75p and can hack at the sacred turf to his heart's content. I will not invite controversy by saying that this is to my mind all wrong.

Even so, you will find that, attached to every public course, there is a club, or clubs, some of them with an inclusive subscription which entitles you to play as often as you like on what is still a public course, others to which you pay a subscription solely for the amenities of the clubhouse. Several clubs in fact surround the rectangle consisting of the first and 18th holes at St. Andrews and of these, foursquare behind the first tee, the senior is the Royal and Ancient. Then there are the New Club, the St. Andrews Club, and for ladies the St. Regulus Club. So, even though you may start at a driving range and graduate to a public course, it is almost certain that you will find yourself joining a club of some sort in the end.

One of the most overworked words in the popular newspapers of today is "exclusive". So-and-so, the gossip columns will say, is a member of the exclusive such-and-such Club. The truth is, of course, that all clubs, whether the Athenaeum or the local British Legion, are exclusive, in that they exclude from membership anyone whom the Committee, representing the members, are unable or unwilling to accept, either because of numbers or for any other reason. Golf clubs are no exception. All, to some degree, are exclusive—though few are as exclusive as they used to be.

Before you join a club, you will almost certainly have played there as a visitor and this will give you a good idea of the general nature and social level of those who are already members. Often it is not only a question of "Will you fit in with them?" Sometimes it is, "Will they fit in with you?" If there is any question of choice, I cannot advise too strongly in favour of joining a club where you will feel socially at home.

As to playing first as a visitor, some clubs still insist that you be introduced by a member and just a few insist, especially at week-ends, that you be actually playing with a member. The vast majority, however, will let you play if you are a member of another club and an increasing proportion will welcome you even if you are not. Apart from stating these facts there is nothing much more that I can do to help.

So it is, too, with actually joining a club. All clubs require you to have a proposer and seconder, but I know many in which, once you have made yourself agreeable as a visitor, the Secretary will be only too pleased to fix matters up. Similarly, if you have started by taking a few lessons from the professional, he will have been able to put you on the right path. Every case has to be treated on its merits. Tactful enquiry will keep you on the right track.

The "explosion" of golf, as it is often called, since the war, has been due, in the more populated parts of England and Scotland, to the "Affluent Society", which in turn has produced literally millions of families who now own motor cars, whereas their parents would never have dreamed of such a thing. This is all very splendid but it does lead to overcrowding, not only of roads and beaches but of golf courses. Golf, when you come to think of it, is based on the motor car. I should think that in the whole of the British Isles not more than one course in ten is readily reached by bicycle or public transport. As more and more people want to play golf and more and more of those who want to play golf own motor cars, the more accessible clubs tend to fill up and it is only reasonable, since there is a limit to the number of people who can play on the course at any given time, that such clubs should proclaim a waiting list.

In this case you must accept, for a while at any rate, an alternative. If you are young and can play only in the holidays from school or university, you may still be able to join the club nearest your home by becoming a five-day member, entitled to use the course only from Monday to Friday, though most clubs will let you use the clubhouse for social purposes on Saturdays and Sundays too.

The older would-be golfer has simply, I am afraid, got to go farther afield. After all, London golfers think nothing of driving 25 or 30 miles each way, perhaps 120 miles all told, in order to play on Saturday and Sunday and, though London is naturally the most difficult of them all, you will probably find that within this distance of most of the crowded cities there are more obscure clubs happy to welcome new members.

What will it cost? Well, I really cannot generalise. Annual subscriptions range from £50 a year downwards to, say, £10 and even less in some parts of Scotland. A fair average for the kind of club the beginner might join would be £20, and in these days of booming golf there might be an entrance fee of the same amount. Nothing ever gets cheaper in life, so one must expect subscriptions to rise rather than fall, as wages, rates and taxes go steadily up. On the other hand it is fair to say that subscriptions, considering what golf and the company of their fellow members mean to most people, have on the whole been kept unrealistically low.

At any rate, whatever club you join, at whatever cost and however far away, I am prepared to bet that you will find it all worth while and be wondering why nobody ever told you about golf before!

vii. Your handicap

PERHAPS the outstanding attraction of golf against other games is, as I mentioned earlier on, the fact that you can play with people much better or much worse than yourself with equal pleasure to both. This is because you have a handicap. This handicap may be anything from scratch (in other words, nought) to 24, or with women players 36, though the fact is that a great many men cannot really play to 24 and a great many women cannot play to 36. One could fill a book double this size with the complicated story, past and present, of golf handicapping, which to me is an immensely dull subject to be left strictly to willing volunteers on the club handicapping committee. Basically, however, it is very simple.

Early in the game's history it became apparent that if you wanted to play with people in other clubs and in other lands, or indeed in competition with members of your own club, some common yardstick had to be found by which to establish a set score for each course upon which everyone's handicap could be based. Thus, if your average goodish round came to, say, 14 strokes over the set score, your handicap would be 14. Your score in a competition might then, though it probably wouldn't, be $86 - 14 = 72$.

The set score for the course has been known successively as the par, the bogey and now the standard scratch score, a ghastly name invented by the national golf Unions, who are in charge of handicapping methods, when they wished to supersede bogey some years before the war. (In 1965 they reintroduced the expression "par" as the set score for each hole but the 18 "pars" did not necessarily add up to the "standard scratch score," on which handicaps are meant to be based. There was such a riot among club golfers at the severity of the new par figures that clubs were "authorised" to fix an easier "bogey" for their members to play against in competitions, though their handicaps were still to be based on the standard scratch score —and, if this has not got you nicely muddled, then I advise you to buy the official booklet. That really will settle it!)

Since handicapping is of such practical day-to-day importance to the golfer, let us go back to the beginning. When I "came in", the set score was known as bogey. The average course would be anything from bogey 70 to 74 and the individual holes bogey 5 or 4 or 3, as the case might be. The bogey at each hole was what a good scratch player, without being one of the very longest hitters in the country, ought to do, allowing him two putts on each green and no mistakes on the way. If he could reach a hole in two, then the bogey was 4; if it took him three (and no hole took more), it was 5; for short holes which he could reach in one, it was 3. This paragon of perfection was christened "Colonel Bogey".

As the game grew in popularity and golfers circulated more amongst each other, two imperfections in this system became apparent. One was that clubs did not fix their bogeys according to any hard and fast rules and a player rated at, say, 12 at one club could play to no better than 16—or, conversely, could play to 8—at another. Human nature being what it is, a good deal of "one-upmanship" went on among neighbouring clubs, each wishing to prove its course superior to the other by making the bogey one stroke higher, and one very famous resort course even declared a bogey of 80, so that visitors went home delighted at having played below their handicaps. Efforts have continually been made to devise a fair and intelligible yardstick by which to fix the set score for all courses and a way, for handicapping purposes, of making allowance for the changing difficulty of the same course from one day to the next. On the whole these have been successful and have been adopted by most clubs.

The other drawback to the original "Colonel Bogey" method was that some courses had quite a number of holes which were undoubtedly out of range in one shot, even for the Colonel at his best, but very easily within range of two—"drive and pitch" holes, as the expression goes—whereas another course might have a great many holes which were undoubtedly within reach of two shots, but only of two really good ones. Each type of hole was, of course, a bogey 4—but a man who could play to his handicap on the former course would be out of his depth on the latter. This, too, has been overcome by a complicated system of allowances for length and such like, which need not in detail concern the newcomer to the game, though, if he cares to master them, he will in no time find himself a very welcome asset to the club handicapping committee!

Of all aspects of golf, handicapping must of necessity be the most imperfect. There is an old golfing story of the man who, after complaining in the club bar that he had been off his game, added an aside: "Come to think of it, I'm never really *on* my game." All the same, we do sometimes have "one of those days"—the kind of day when we hit one out of bounds into the railway line and it hits a rail and bounces back into play, and when the long putt that was going miles past the hole hits the back, jumps up and drops in. Perhaps it happens during a competition. Is our handicap to be based on this single best score? It would be unfair if it were, since we might only play to our handicap once in a year, and then only on our home course.

The ideal would be if everyone took out a card every time he played and marked his score on it—which is what happens in America. The committee would then have a permanent, up-to-date record of our progress, or otherwise. The club golfer, however, seems to be a different kind of animal on this side of the Atlantic and, unless he is playing in a stroke competition, nothing will induce him to put in a card. What is more, tens of thousands of players never put in a card at all, remaining perhaps at 15-handicap for many years after they have ceased to be able to play to 20. Still, it all seems to work out agreeably and so long as members of the club are handicapped roughly correctly in relationship to each other most people are happy.

As to the beginner, it should be a matter of pride, I think, especially for young people, to obtain a handicap as soon as possible and to reduce it as far and as quickly as your talent allows. Instinct will tell you when you have become as good as you are likely to get and it is then a question of holding on till the time comes—all too soon, alas—when you know that your handicap will never do anything but go steadily up.

In stroke competitions the manner of using your handicap is simple. You add up your score and deduct your handicap from the total. In match play, however, a complication arises. To quote the invaluable Golfer's Handbook, "The handicaps for match play are based on the number of strokes which players receive in stroke play, but only a proportion is allowed in match play. The reason for this is that an inferior player is more uncertain than a scratch player, but his mistakes are less disastrous to him in match than they are in stroke play. Thus in match play a 15-handicap player may take 8 to a hole which his scratch opponent does in 3, but the latter thereby only gains one hole and not five strokes as he would in stroke play."

So the answer is that in match play the higher-handicap man receives only three-quarters of the difference between his and his opponent's handicap. Fractions of half a stroke or over count as one stroke; less than half, nothing. Thus, if you are 10 and I am 16, in playing in a stroke competition we simply deduct 10 and 16 from our respective totals, but playing against each other in ordinary day-to-day club golf you give me three-quarters of six, namely four and a half, which, fortunately for me, counts five. If you had been 10 and I had been 15, it would have been $4\frac{1}{4}$, in other words 4.

I receive my strokes, one at a time, at holes nominated on the card of the course on which we are playing. Generally the committee nominate that the first stroke shall come at a hole —not too late in the round, in case the game is over—which they deem most difficult to do in the par figure, in other words where the lesser player has most need of a little help. Nowadays one does not necessarily have to consult the card, since most clubs put figures on the tee boxes showing whether this is a "stroke hole". Thus, if you see on a tee box, one above the other, the figures 10 385 4 12 you know that this is the 10th hole; that it is 385 yards long; that the par is 4; and that, if you are receiving 12 strokes *or more*, you get one here. If you are only receiving 11, no luck!

There are, of course, different forms of fractional allowances for foursomes, fourballs, Stableford competitions and the rest, but I do not think we need go into them here. One other form of handicap I should perhaps mention, however, because it can lead to excellent fun and may be the medium of splendid and prolonged haggling before the game begins. This is the "bisque". In the normal way you take your strokes where the card says. You may, at a vital "stroke hole", become involved in a gorse bush and throw your stroke away. Alternatively, and in a way even more exasperating, your opponent, who is conceding a stroke, may himself become involved in a gorse bush, so that you would have won the hole anyway. A bisque on the other hand is a certainty. You take it when and where you like, when the hole is finished.

You can take two at one hole if you are in dire straits and if you have them to spare. The more unreliable a player you are, the more valuable is a bisque by comparison with a stroke which has to be taken at a given hole. Psychology comes into it too. Do you, for instance, take a precious bisque to halve the first hole instead of losing it? You know perfectly well that it can never make any greater difference later on, but every instinct tells you to "save it up". Many a good golfer, intelligent enough in other spheres, has had the mortification of being beaten with several bisques in hand, unable to use them because he has left it too late and is now stuck in the gorse bush!

There are, of course, other forms of handicap, or giving of odds, that have been devised by crafty and ingenious golfers, but I end this chapter as I began, by saying that it is the possession of a handicap that makes golf unique among games. With the aid of it you can play with anyone, at any age, anywhere in the world.

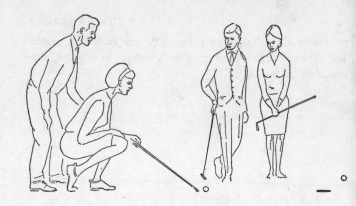

viii. Forms of play and club competitions

IT is possible to play round a golf course entirely by yourself and sometimes, if the course is clear, a beginner likes to plough a lonely furrow in this way in order to make his early hesitant attempts away from the public gaze. This is a phase, which, if you ever do go through it, should not be allowed to last. Solo golf is not much fun and you would be better employed in hitting a greater number of shots with a bucket of balls on the practice ground or at a driving range, in a much shorter time and preferably with someone to give a helping hand. If you do play alone—and, golf being the sociable game that it is, practically nobody ever does—remember that a single player has, as the saying is, "no standing on the course" and *must* let players coming along behind pass through. Just wave them on and stand aside. In one very lush country club which I visited in California they had about 200 electric carts in the "buggy stables" and drove round the course in them, as a result of which they had perhaps the most remarkable single rule in the history of golf, namely that players *on foot* had no standing on the course!

The normal forms of play are fourballs, singles, threeballs and foursomes—in that order of popularity. In the United States almost all club golfers play fourballs. They cheerfully take anything up to $5\frac{1}{2}$ hours and it drives me personally round the bend. In Britain, as the game becomes more crowded, it is only natural that fourball golf should be the order of the day, since, although four people take longer than two, you can still get a great many more people round the course in a given time if they play in fours.

In this country we tend to regard golf as essentially a match play game—apart from certain forms of competition, to which I shall refer in due course. It may be of interest, however, to note in passing that right from the beginning of golf in their country the Americans have looked on it as a stroke play game. When four of us in this country assemble for a game of golf, we tend to say "You and I will take on the other two" and then start haggling about how many strokes they ought to give us, especially in view of the fact that neither of us has played for a long time and both have had colds. The American club golfer says, logically enough, that he has come out to play 18 holes of golf and to see how many he can get round in, or "shoot". He therefore holes out at every hole, marking his score on a card, and five hours later settles down in the "men's grill" to match his card for dollars and cents with about sixteen other people's.

In this country the fourball is a partnership affair, "us against them", and if at any hole one partner has already secured a figure which the other one cannot better, it is regarded as rather bad form and "holding up the course" for the other one to carry on and hole out in order to see how many strokes he can complete the hole in. This is the great weakness of fourball golf and the main reason, apart from the time element, why older-fashioned golfers like myself tend to avoid it like the plague. It is infuriating, just when the play of the hole is reaching its most interesting stage, i.e., on or in the neighbourhood of the green, to become suddenly "out of it" because your partner has played a good shot and you therefore cannot improve upon his score for the hole. Nevertheless, for the strictly week-end golfer who wants to enjoy the company of his own cronies in not too strenuous circumstances, fourballs are the thing and this in most clubs is the customary form of Sunday morning golf.

Threeballs are more rare but to me represent a good form of golf. Far from many of your shots in a fourball not counting at all—sometimes not even being played—every shot in a threeball, all on your own against two separate opponents, counts twice. You can, of course, play separate matches, each against the other two, but the best way is the six-points-per-hole system, which is extremely simple, though it is never so easy to convey these things on paper as in person. At each hole six points are available to be won: 4 to the man with the best score, 2 to the second, 0 to the third. If all three have the same score, each gets two points, so there is no change from the previous position. So the scores for a hole may be 4, 2, 0: or 4, 1, 1: or 3, 3, 0: or 2, 2, 2. The great thing is to adjust the total score at the end of each hole so that for simplicity the last man stays at 0. So instead of getting up to, let us say, 22, 16, 10, you keep it down to 12, 6, 0, which relatively is the same thing. If the total number of points do not add up to a multiple of six, you are in trouble. Get it straightened out before you play the next hole. If the handicaps are reasonable, there is rarely any spectacular difference at the end and to play for sixpence or a shilling a point adds much to the fun and has never ruined anyone yet.

After the fourball the most "normal" form of golf is, I suppose, the single—simply a straightforward match between yourself and the other man, played on handicap, and on the basis not of how many strokes you take but of holes won and lost, i.e., with a 4 against a 5 counting "one up" in just the same way as a 4 against a 7. When you are, say, 4 up with 3 to play, you are home and dry and the remaining three holes constitute the bye—on which, should he care, the loser has the traditional right of wagering half the original stake. This applies, of course, not only to singles but to all forms of match play.

Finally, I should perhaps say a word about foursomes, in which two players hit one ball alternately, one player driving off at the odd holes and the other at the even, irrespective of which one played the last stroke on the hole before. This form of game is unknown in America except in international matches against the British and is referred to as a "Scotch foursome". In Britain it is a game largely for the connoisseur and I dare say ninety per cent of all players go through their golfing lives without ever playing one. Nevertheless, "foursomes in the morning, singles in the afternoon" is the accepted form in events like the four-cornered internationals between England, Ireland, Scotland and Wales; the University match, and matches between senior clubs. I will say no more than that the foursome is a truly wonderful form of golf and no one has known the full savour of the game until he has tried it.

There is also, highly to be commended, a variation between

49

the fourball and the foursome known as a greensome (invented by Sir Lycett Green, of Norfolk), in which all four players drive at each hole and then, picking the better of the two drives, continue as a foursome, the non-driver of the ball chosen playing the second shot. A further and perhaps even better variation starts, as before, with everyone playing from the tee and then, so that it shall not turn out that player A seems to play an undue proportion of the second shots, he plays the second shot at all the odd holes (either with his own drive or his partner's) while B plays the second at all the even holes. Both games are excellent. They avoid the tedium of the fourball but at the same time get over the main trouble with the foursome for the week-end golfer, namely, that he may have to get a good many bad shots out of his system before he gets going, any one of which may completely spoil the hole for both him and his partner in a foursome.

Competitions

There are three forms of competition in club golf and the moment you reach the stage of gaining a handicap you should "have a go". It is all good fun: you meet different people: it sharpens up your golf by showing you up in your true image; and nobody in the world, except perhaps yourself, cares if you don't do any good.

These club competitions may be stroke play, knock-out match play, or "Stableford". The first, also known as medal play, has grown less and less popular in club golf—though professional tournaments, with only two exceptions, are by stroke play. Many clubs still hold a Monthly Medal and among the senior ones there is often an actual Gold Medal of some antiquity which is annually contested, sometimes over two rounds instead of one. One such is the handsome King William IV Medal presented to the Royal and Ancient Golf

Club of St. Andrews by His Majesty in 1837 and played for by the members at the autumn meeting. Three years later Queen Adelaide presented the club with another exquisite Medal. This is "won" by the new captain as he drives himself into office and he wears it on all public occasions.

Among indifferent golfers, which in fact means about eighty per cent, competitions by stroke play are unpopular because one "disaster", which is as likely to occur at the first hole as any other, perhaps more so, can put him completely out of the hunt. His score is ruined but as his playing partner is still keeping his own score there is not even a match for him to play. The whole round has lost its interest. Thus a more popular form of club tournament, known as a bogey competition, was instituted a long time ago, wherein each player played a match against "Colonel Bogey", i.e., the score on the card, receiving strokes at certain holes according to his handicap. The only difference between this and an ordinary match was that it was played to the end, with no bye, so that instead of, say, winning by 4 and 3 you would play on to the 18th and could finish in that case anything from 7 up to 1 up according to how you fared at the last three holes.

Gradually people came to feel that this too had an obvious shortcoming. The man who got a 5, say, at a bogey-4 hole surely deserved something a little better than the man who took 7. At this point there stepped into golfing immortality Dr. Frank Stableford, of Wallasey, who in 1931 devised the simple scheme of awarding 2 points for a bogey and one point for one over. You also, though more rarely, get 3 points for a score of one under bogey, 4 for two under and, I suppose, 5 for 3 under—which would mean holing your second shot at a long bogey-five hole. Thus, receiving your handicap strokes against bogey wherever marked on the card, you are still in the hunt if you take 7 at a bogey-5 or 6 at a bogey-4, provided that you are in receipt of a stroke at that hole, e.g. 7 less 1 = 6, which is one over bogey and counts 1 point. In my opinion this is far and away the best form of club competition and, if knighthoods were awarded for golf, the late Dr. Stableford, for all the pleasure he gave, and is still giving, should have had one.

Many clubs run a knock-out competition lasting some months, of which perhaps the most congenial form is the Winter Foursomes, helping to brighten up the shorter days of winter, but perhaps one of the most neglected forms of "keeping up the interest" is what used in my younger days to be called an Eclectic competition and is now known at clubs all over the United States as a "Ringer". It will last for perhaps three months. Every player has 18 spaces after his name on a big board and, when he does a worthwhile score at a hole, he enters it up and puts a ring round it. As time goes on, he accumulates a 2 at most of the short holes, 4s at most of the long holes and so on, and in this way it lends continuous interest even when you are playing badly. You never know when a lucky break is going to give you "one for the ringer" and excitement as the time limit draws near becomes intense.

ix. The rules

IN earlier days the Rules of golf were very simple. In 1860, for instance, there were only twelve, most of them stated in one or two lines. As the game progressed, however, and became more sophisticated, the situations in which golfers found themselves and sought guidance from the Rules multiplied, and so, gradually, did the Rules. Now the little booklet in which they are set out—though let not the beginner be unduly dismayed by this—runs to no fewer than 93 pages. Nor is this all, for there are also innumerable Decisions upon the Rules, the result of the hundreds of queries sent up to the Royal and Ancient by intelligent people who still cannot reach a conclu-

sion from the original 93 pages. Almost everyone will agree
that the Rules of golf, like the laws relating to taxation, are of
such bewildering complexity that the best thing to do would
be to scrap the lot and start over again. This is more easily
said than done. An effort has, however, been made and I shall
come to it in a moment.

If we did start again, we should go back first of all to the
original basic rule of golf *"The ball shall be played where it
lies."* Golf, before it reached its present complications, was
more of an adventure. Courses, and particularly greens, had
not acquired their present "manicured" perfection and there
was a lot more taking of the rough with the smooth. Where
the ball lay, there you played it. If you could not play it, you
lost the hole and that was that.

It was the understandable erosion of this basic rule that
began the present complications. People who had to work
during the week and had only the week-ends for their golf
did not want to forfeit the hole and the fun of playing it
simply because their drive lay unplayable in a bush or was
lost on the railway line. They were happy enough to accept a
penalty, but they wanted to be able to play on. So there arose
more and more circumstances in which you could, in the
current phrase, "obtain relief"—in other words, move your
ball, sometimes with a penalty of two strokes, sometimes one,
sometimes none. On the whole this is for the greatest good of
the greatest number but it does, as I say, tend to make life
complicated.

Perhaps I might offer an observation on the attitude of,
I am sure, 99 out of 100 golfers towards the Rules. Golf is, I
suppose, a comparatively easy game at which to cheat—to
improve the lie of the ball, perhaps, or fail to count an un-
observed stroke. This is perhaps why cheating is so remark-
ably rare that, when detected, it is more likely to make a

comical story than a serious one. Among my favourite golfing stories, for instance, is that of a Cambridge University player just before my day who was well known to cheat—largely because he played for more money than he could afford. An old friend of mine, Dale Bourn, who won the English championship in 1930, told me how he was partnering this character in the foursomes against the West Hill club and at the last hole drove their ball into a deep bunker. He arrived to find his partner surreptitiously teeing it up in the sand. "Oh, I say . . ." he said, or words to that effect—to which the man looked up from the bunker and said, "What? They didn't see me, did they?"

Some time ago, endeavouring to prove (and, as I like to think, doing so) that a perfectly adequate code of Rules for the club golfer could be condensed to go on the back of a score card, I concluded with the words, "ensuring, as always, that no advantage to himself shall accrue". There is a major difference between golf and more active sports. Only the other day I was sitting among a gathering of really distinguished ex-cricketers and found them deeply and sincerely divided on the question of whether a batsman should "walk" when he thought he was out—one side saying firmly that he should, the other maintaining that what mattered was what the umpire said and that it was an insult to anticipate his decision. I mention this only to emphasise that in golf you are batsman and umpire in one. If you think you are out, you walk! The immortal Bobby Jones, who in 1930 made the Grand Slam—winning the open and amateur championships of Britain and the United States all in the same year—"called" a penalty stroke on himself, his ball having moved a fraction of an inch as he addressed it, when this additional stroke might well have cost him the U.S. Open.

All the same it is fair to say that, human nature being what it is, you will find some golfers who will sail near to the wind simply in order to win, but they generally have a reputation as such and are to be avoided. The real villainy occurs not so much in direct action on the course as in deliberate "farming" of their handicap and it is my experience that, the moment there exists a selling sweep running into, say, hundreds of pounds, otherwise honest men will get up to all sorts of tricks to inflate their handicaps. It is some years, however, before the reader will be venturing forth into that sort of company!

For the moment I would suggest only that you become familiar with what you may do in the more normal eventualities in a round of golf, bearing in mind the ancient principle that the ball must be "played where it lies", unless the Rules permit otherwise. What happens, for instance, if it is lost, or finishes out of bounds, or unplayable, or up against a brick wall or—as did Harry Bradshaw's in the 1949 Open championship at Sandwich, thus possibly costing him the title—in a broken beer bottle?

Luckily a former Chairman of the Rules of Golf Committee and of the Golf Foundation, Mr. Gerald Micklem, appreciating the complexity of the complete code of Rules for the average club golfer, formulated an abbreviated version entitled "Some Guidance to the Rules of Golf". This is shaped like a score card and will fit easily into the pocket of any golf bag, and furthermore is written in straightforward, as against "legal", English. Copies of this invaluable little document may be had in any quantity, absolutely free, from the Golf Foundation, 2 St. James Square, London, S.W.1, and I cannot too strongly recommend the beginner to get hold of one, either from the Foundation or from a club Secretary, thus settling once and for all everything he is likely to need concerning the Rules of Golf. As a matter of interest, its contents are appended below but do please get the card itself, so as to have it with you when you play.

SOME GUIDANCE TO THE RULES OF GOLF

Since the Game of Golf is not played in a small defined area with a single moving ball, the Rules are necessarily more complicated than in most other games. The Golf Foundation have therefore prepared the following summary of some of the basic Rules with which the new player should be familiar in even his earliest rounds. It is stressed that only the briefest outline is given. And while this summary has the whole-hearted approval of the Rules of Golf Committee of the Royal and Ancient Golf Club, it cannot be applied in settling any dispute which may arise in play; for that purpose the text of the official Rules must always be referred to.

This summary is accordingly in no sense a substitute for the Rules themselves, which every player should study. In particular, the attention of players entering for competitions or matches is drawn to Rules 36 and 37.

Ball Played as It Lies

You must play the ball as it lies, unless the Rules allow you to do otherwise.

Improving Lie Prohibited

You must not press down anything which would improve your lie: but outside a hazard you may remove loose impediments such as leaves, loose branches and twigs, wormcasts, provided that the ball does not move during or after their removal. You may not improve your line of play, your lie or the area of your intended swing, by moving, breaking or bending anything growing except in *fairly* taking your stance or in making your stroke.

Wrong Ball

There are penalties for playing someone else's ball (except in a hazard), so put a mark on your ball to help you identify it.

Ball at Rest Moved

If you move your ball accidentally, you must play it as it lies under penalty of one stroke.

Ball Lost, Out of Bounds or Unplayable

If you cannot find your ball after looking for it for five minutes, if you abandon it as lost, with or without searching for it, or if you hit it out of bounds, you must play your next stroke from where you played the original stroke, counting that stroke and adding a penalty stroke to your score (this penalty is known as "stroke and distance").

If you hit your ball into what you consider is an unplayable lie, you may drop the ball, adding one penalty stroke, either within two club-lengths of the unplayable spot, but not nearer the hole, or anywhere directly behind it; alternatively, you may play another stroke, as in the previous paragraph, with penalty of stroke and distance.

Provisional Ball

If you think that your ball may be lost or out of bounds, to save time, you may play a provisional ball from the original spot before going forward, and you may go on playing this ball, until you reach the place where the original ball is likely to be. If then you find your original ball in bounds and playable you must pick up the provisional one; if the original ball is lost or out of bounds, you may continue with the provisional ball with the penalty or stroke and distance as in the first paragraph of the previous section.

If however your original ball is in bounds, but unplayable, you may not continue with your provisional ball, but proceed with either of the alternatives in the second paragraph of the previous section, i.e. dropping under penalty of one stroke or going back to the original spot with stroke and distance penalty.

Obstructions

An obstruction is something *artificial* erected or placed on the Course, but does not include fences and walls marking out of bounds.

If the obstruction interferes with your play and is movable, you may move it.

If it is immovable, and if it interferes with your stance or intended swing, then you may drop your ball two club-lengths from the point on the outside of the obstruction nearest which it lay, but not nearer the hole, without penalty.

Casual Water, Ground under Repair, Hole made by a Burrowing Animal

Casual water is any *temporary* accumulation of water.

Ground under repair is any part of the Course so marked, and includes material such as grass mowings piled for removal, even is not so marked.

If your ball lies or is lost in, or your stance or swing is interfered with by casual water, ground under repair or a hole made by a burrowing animal, you may drop the ball two club-lengths away from the affected area, but not nearer the hole, without penalty.

If this situation arises when your ball is in a hazard, then you may drop *in* the hazard *without* penalty, or *behind* the hazard under penalty of *one stroke*.

If your ball is on the green, and these conditions interfere, or intervene between your ball and the hole, you may *place* the ball *on the nearest spot* avoiding these conditions, not nearer the hole.

Hazards and Water Hazards

When your ball is in a bunker or a water hazard, you may not, before making a stroke, touch the ground or water with your club in addressing the ball or in any other way, nor may you test the condition of the bunker, except that you may take a firm stance. You may not touch or move a loose impediment in a hazard.

When your ball is anywhere in a water hazard, you may drop it as far behind the hazard as you wish, keeping the spot where it entered the hazard between yourself and the hole, under penalty of one stroke, or you may play another stroke from where you played the original stroke under penalty of stroke and distance.

When your ball is in a lateral water hazard, which means that it is impossible to drop behind as above, then you may drop within two club-lengths on either side under penalty of one stroke.

The Flagstick

You may always have the flagstick attended, removed, or held up to indicate the position of the hole, but you must decide on this before you play your stroke; the flagstick is entirely under your control.

If your ball strikes the flagstick, when attended, or, if played from the putting green strikes it when attended or unattended, you lose the hole in match play and suffer a penalty of two strokes in medal play.

The Putting Green

You may clean your ball on the green.

You may repair pitch marks on the green.

If your opponent's ball interferes with your play, you may ask him to lift it.

If in match play your ball strikes your opponent's ball, he may replace it or play it from where it lies at his option, and you suffer no penalty: but if in medal play both balls are on the putting green, there is a two stroke penalty for striking the other ball, which must be replaced.

You may not play the ball on the green with a stance astride the line of your putt in the manner of a croquet player.

Undue Delay

You must at all times play without undue delay.

x. Etiquette

GOLF is essentially a do-it-yourself game. You therefore
expect to be allowed to get on with it without interference
from your opponent, your partner or anyone else. Such interference may be mental or physical and you may take it from
me that the former is the more deadly of the two. "Gamesmanship" and golf go hand in hand.

The official "Etiquette" is stated in rather formal terms,
or so I always think; but all it comes down to is good manners.
Perhaps the most important single item in golfing good manners is self-effacement. When a man is concentrating on a golf
shot, he is conscious, or wishes to be, of nothing else. It is up

to you to ensure that you do not in any way intrude upon this "unconsciousness". While he is lining up for his shot, as well as while he is actually playing it, you should stand out of sight and absolutely still, either opposite him or well behind his back, but never in any circumstances behind his line of play, where the slightest movement will divert his eye. Taking practice swings while it is his turn to play, especially on the green, is another familiar nuisance of which most of us find ourselves guilty at some time or other. Not, I trust, on purpose, though I am afraid it has been known to happen that way, the chief offender in my own experience having been a well-known member of Parliament, at that.

Some people are more "touchy" than others, particularly in so infuriating a pastime as golf, and I hope I may say, without appearing to be preaching a sermon, that it is up to each of us to make allowances for the other man's foibles. Some people like to talk a good deal as they go round. Lloyd George, for instance, thought golf "much the best game. It takes place in the open air, you play with beauty all around you, you get exercise, and you can talk all the time." Others are intent with their own thoughts and, if they do not talk a great deal during a round of golf, it does not mean that they are being unsociable. They will "unwind" in the bar afterwards and this after all is where golf and talk go best together.

Some people, again, are more easily put off than others. There was the P. G. Wodehouse character who declared himself put off by the intolerable "uproar of the butterflies in the adjacent meadow". Another man, missing a very short putt on the 6th green at Deal, which is right beside the foreshore, raised his club aloft and cried "How the devil can a man be expected to putt with all this traffic going up and down the Channel!" The late and great Bernard Darwin, the best writer on golf, perhaps on any game, that ever lived, was of an extremely testy disposition on the links. All we can do with the more sensitive golfer is to ensure that, if he is going to be put off, it is certainly not going to be by us.

The easiest golfer to put off is the one who is doing particularly well and this has many a time been done on purpose by the less scrupulous among us. The first principle of Stephen Potter's "Gamesmanship", it will be remembered, is "Break the flow". If the other man is doing too well, the best way of breaking the flow, in golf at any rate, is to keep reminding him how well he is doing. A suggestion that he is hitting the ball farther than usual is also an almost certain means of making him "press" and therefore of destroying the rhythm of his swing. The merest hint that "surely he has changed his grip" or "seems to be taking his putter back more along the ground"—almost anything, however trivial, will "break the flow".

However, this is not the moment to write at length on the dodges by which golfers throughout the ages have continued to get "one up" on the other man, so I will merely append "Some Points of Golf Etiquette", which follows the Guidance to the Rules of Golf previously quoted. Let me say once again that, so far as golf is concerned, Etiquette is simply another word for good manners, adding only that the worst of bad manners is to spoil the day of the people playing behind you by keeping them waiting. If the pace of the course is slow and you yourself are kept waiting by the people in front, well and good. The people behind will appreciate that there is nothing you can do about it. Golf is a leisurely game and no one expects you to run round the course, but, if you find yourselves losing ground on the people in front, it is a matter of good manners and therefore of golfing etiquette to *get a move on*.

SOME POINTS ON GOLF ETIQUETTE

You, and the people who play with you, will enjoy the game of golf much more if you follow these simple rules of etiquette:—

Don't play until the match in front of you is out of range, but don't delay your own game.

If you are overtaken by other players while you are looking for a lost ball, or because of your own slow play, call the other players on, then wait until they are out of range before you continue your own game.

Don't move, talk, stand close to or directly behind the ball or the hole when a player is making a stroke.

Fill in all the holes and footmarks you may make in the bunker sand. And see that any "divots" you may cut up are replaced and pressed down.

Don't take your golf cart on to tees or greens, or any other area from which carts are banned.

Don't damage the greens—marks made by your shoes or the flagstick may deflect well-aimed putts. Greens are often rather soft so stand well away from the cup and hold the flag so that it doesn't mark the green.

Don't flick the ball out of the hole with the blade of your putter.

And when you've finished putting, don't loiter on the green; there are other people waiting to play.

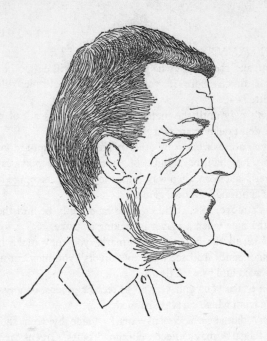

xi. "Simple Golf" by Peter Thomson

A few years ago I played in a practice round before a professional–amateur tournament in the distinguished company of Peter Thomson, of Australia, five times winner of the British Open, and the late Ian Fleming, creator of James Bond. I was very bad. Naturally enough, I turned to the expert. "There must be *something* I can do about it!" I remember saying. Thomson's reply was immediate. "Well," he said, "you're set up all wrong, for a start." So he got me "set up" right—a favourite expression of his—and, though it seemed to pull a lot of muscles which ought to have been, but had not been, used over the past few years and was altogether rather painful at first, there was not the slightest doubt about it that he was right. Fleming and I both got ourselves "set up right" and our game improved from that moment. Furthermore, one *knew* that Thomson was right.

As a result of this episode Fleming enthused about Thomson's ideas on golf in the office of *The Sunday Times,* of which he was then foreign editor, and it was suggested that I might get these ideas out of him for the benefit of our readers. We therefore had two half-hour sessions together at St. Andrews during the open championship and as a result of these two short meetings there emerged what I still think is just about the best, and certainly the most succinct, piece of golfing instruction I have ever read. Nor is there any lack of modesty in this assertion, since, as you will see, Thomson's contribution is everything and the writer's virtually nothing. When Thomson won the Open at Birkdale four years later, *The Sunday Times* reprinted these two pieces, and innumerable people cut them out and filed them away for reference against a rainy day. So here now is Peter Thomson's "Simple Way to Good Golf" and I am grateful both to *The Sunday Times* and, in particular, to Thomson himself for permission to reprint what follows.

"This expression, 'getting set up right', constitutes the absolute basis of Thomson's golf. 'If you get set up right and look like a competent golfer, you won't go nearly so far wrong.' Your set-up consists of how you stand, where you are aiming, your 'triangle' (i.e., the two arms and shoulders), and where you put the ball in relation to your feet.

"The nearer you are, before you start, to the position in which you will be when you hit the ball, the fewer adjustments you will have to make in the course of the shot. 'Think how your body has to be when you strike the ball,' he says, 'and work back from there.' Lest this sounds too obvious, take a look on the first tee on a Sunday morning and see how many people's starting position bears any relation to any position in which they could conceivably be at impact!

"There is no reason why any of us, tall or short, fat or thin, should not get set up right. The stance, about which volumes have been written, is a piece of typical Thomsonian simplicity. Lay a club down on the ground, pointing to the hole, and put your toes against it. That is the end of that.

"Now put the ball opposite your left foot with your left arm and the club in a straight line, as they will be, or should be, as you actually hit the ball. Your arm and the club will now be at right-angles to the imaginary club on the ground against which you have lined up your toes. If they are not, you have got the ball—*as almost everyone has*—too far back. (We are talking at the moment of wooden club shots.)

"We now come to the critical point, the make-or-mar of the entire set-up. Your right arm is not long enough. It won't reach. How are you going to get it on to the club?

"You do it instinctively as nature tells you, the easiest way. You reach over with the right hand, bringing the right shoulder forward in the process, and at the same time probably without realising it you bring the left hand back a bit to meet it. You then reach a position which is perfectly comfortable but, to make it more so, you probably move forward a couple of inches at the last moment, thus, in effect, bringing the ball two inches back. The whole set-up is now wrecked.

"Let us go back, if we may, to the original position. The right arm once again is not long enough. This time, keeping your right shoulder back and tilting your left shoulder up, you reach under with the right hand and attach it to the club. You then reach a position in which—I don't care what you say—you at least *look* like a golfer.

"I tried this experiment on many willing subjects and in every case, regardless of handicap, in position 3 they at once looked like a golfer. If it feels awkward at first, it only shows how wrong you were before. You can apply a simple test. When you have got 'set up', keep your body still, lay the club flat across your chest and see where it is pointing. In the second, or wrong, position you will find it points yards to the left of the hole. In the correct set-up it will be pointing straight at the flag.

"HOW FAR AWAY FROM THE BALL SHOULD YOU BE? Thomson often uses the expression 'measuring off'. You will notice that he himself measures off quite deliberately before each shot. Stand relaxed, leaning slightly forward, with your knees slightly bent and the whole body *in balance*. Extend the left arm and the club in a straight line, not stiff as a ramrod, and you are now measured off. 'Picture in mind your position as you strike the ball and make final adjustments from that.' This applies to every club.

"HOW DO YOU GRIP THE CLUB? Again, delightfully simple. *Get set up right and you won't notice!* Take it as you find it.

"HOW HARD DO YOU HOLD ON TO THE CLUB? 'Often,' says Thomson, 'you can actually *see* the tension in a man's hand. You should start with a light touch, barely enough to lift it off the ground—so that it feels heavy. It is just like using an axe. You lift it with a light grip, just enough to raise it, and it feels heavy. As you bring it down, your grip tightens without your thinking about it and reaches its tightest at the moment of impact.

" 'There is another likeness with golf. Using an axe, you do not *hit* with it; you *accelerate* it. That is exactly what you should do with a golf club.'

"HOW DO YOU START THE CLUB BACK? 'Well,

you just *draw it straight back*. Never mind about what the books din into you about turns and pivots. Just draw it straight back as far as is comfortable and let nature take its course. Don't turn away: just draw it back —*but*—keep your weight squarely on both feet and make sure you don't sway back with it yourself.'

"Finally, what Thomson describes as the key axiom in the golf swing, namely, to be *behind* the ball when you strike it—not all of you, maybe, but certainly your head. 'A plumb line from your nose as you strike the ball should hit the ground several inches behind it'—a sobering thought for us lurchers and swayers, to whom, as we heave forward, the ball so often appears to be moving rapidly backwards.

"As a postscript I might add that, with the first shot in which Thomson was satisfied that he had got me satisfactorily 'setup', I ricked my back—probably using muscles which had not come into play for 30 years—to such an extent that we almost had to terminate the game there and then. This in no way shook my faith in his principles and I wish you the best of luck. You have been warned!

"When I described the emphasis placed by Peter Thomson on how important it is to get 'set up' right before making a golf shot, the example taken was a wooden club shot, but the same principle applies to all.

"We are to imagine the position in which we shall, or ought to be, when we hit the ball and set ourselves up as nearly in that position as possible. It will involve, as always, the left arm and the club in a straight line, rather as though one were about to play a one-armed shot with the left arm.

"The position of the ball with the driver was simple. It was opposite the left foot. Where is it to be with the other clubs? Again there are no complications. His answer is 'roughly an inch farther back for each club'. This finds the ball midway between the feet with a 5-iron and about off the right heel with a 9-iron. With the driver you hit the teed-up ball an ascending blow, the club head having already passed its lowest point. With the short irons you hit it a descending blow, taking a good-sized divot after the ball.

"HOW FAR AWAY DO YOU STAND? Again the same principles apply throughout. You 'measure off'—another favourite expression—with the left arm extended, and yourself poised and in balance but naturally stooping a little more with the shorter clubs than you did with the driver.

"Thomson also likes to have his feet progressively closer together as the shots become shorter. It all seems to fit into a very simple and intelligible pattern. As the shots become short enough to require judgment rather than power for their execution, he likes to open the stance slightly drawing his left foot back a little.

"For the short game his maxim, typically, is that one should always look for the *simplest* way. He describes the high wedge shot, which we so much admire when played by professionals, as, for most people, 'a form of lunacy'. The more you can picture a short approach as a kind of extended putt, he says, the better.

"The ruin of most handicap players' short game comes from their efforts to hit the ball *up*. It is the golfer's job to hit it *forwards*, the lofted club's job to hit *upwards*. It is an old professional trick, in trying to teach this to beginners, to put a lofted club into their hands and invite them to try to hit the ball along the ground into a bunker between them and the flag. They concentrate on hitting the ball forwards, whereupon it sails over the bunker.

"Thomson is a supremely good bunker player. Perhaps his finest exhibition of this art was when he won the Open at Lytham in 1958, where they have innumerable bunkers, of which he encountered at least his share. I have always remembered his remark afterwards that he had 'never seen such beautiful sand'. He sincerely regards 'splashing' the ball out of sand as the simplest shot in the whole game, if only because there is so much greater a margin for error than with a similar shot off grass.

" 'The chief factor is the club itself. There are some atrocious old sand-irons about that even Snead could not play with. You want one with a wide sole, with the back edge considerably lower than the front.' He thinks little or nothing of most of the so-called 'dual purpose' clubs.

"He reckons to stand well behind the ball and to 'measure off' carefully to the exact point that he wishes to hit the sand. Instead of hitting the ball first and the turf afterwards, you hit the sand first and the ball afterwards. You can hit the sand anything from two to six inches behind and it may well be sometimes that the clubface never actually touches the ball at all. So far as you are concerned at any rate, you are playing a shot at the sand rather than at the ball. His only golden rule is 'Swing very slowly.'

"Thomson is also—again in an unostentatious and 'simple' way—a supremely good putter. I spent a long time drawing him out on the subject and from this I think three main points emerge. He does not think that the grip matters unduly—indeed he used the words 'almost any grip will do'—but he has no doubt about his own method.

"To initiate it, take a normal grip, then rotate your left hand to the left so that the back of it is at about 45 degrees to the ground; do likewise with your right hand to the right, and then stick your right thumb firmly on the shaft. He also reckons to stand with his eyes vertically over the ball. All this is common ground but there are many who might vastly improve by giving it a trial.

"His second point interested me because I have so often

referred to it as one of the main secrets of Locke's phenomenally successful putting and because it is something that we can all so easily do and, even when we mean to, so often don't. It is to carry out a sort of *drill*: in other words to find a set of motions that suits our own particular eye and temperament and carry them out, without exception, every time we putt.

"For his third point I quote his own words. 'It must incorporate some sort of *determined tap*. What kills putting is the old so-called "stroking" method. You don't stroke a putt like you stroke a cat. If you do, it is usually timid and damned lucky if it goes in the hole. The most natural way is to give it a tap, like a child instinctively does.'

"He named as the world's best putters Rosburg, Casper, Ford, Palmer and Venturi—all Americans who hit the ball with a firm tap rather than a smooth stroking movement. This, I need hardly add, is not to be confused with a quick jerk or jab!

"Like Locke, Thomson thinks it essential to hold the club loosely with a very light, sensitive grip and likes to have the *feeling* that he is playing the same stroke every time, increasing the length more by lengthening the backswing than by hitting harder."

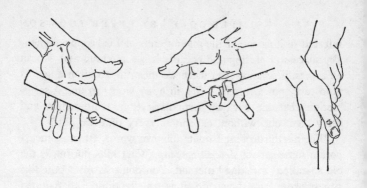

xii. Hints and tips

I have written in this book, and indeed have been writing all my life, that the best way to get started in golf is to invest in a few lessons with a professional, whether at the nearest club, an indoor school or a driving range. Nevertheless, watching the game and its best players for so long has convinced me that there are certain hints, tips and "short cuts" which may save the beginner a great deal of time, and some of these I am going to venture to pass on.

The first is blindingly simple, and yet many people go through an entire golfing lifetime without thinking of it, at any rate in this simple form, namely that it is the golfer's job to hit the ball *forwards*. It is the job of the *club*, not of the golfer, to cause it to fly *upwards*. The degree of "upwardness" depends, of course, on the loft of the face of the club with which you hit it forwards. Let me quote an example from table tennis, which I am sure every reader has played at some time or other. You have a stationary ball on your side of the table and you wish to flip it over the net to your opponent for him to serve with. What do you do? You lay the face of the bat back and slide it sharply forwards *along the surface of the table*. Up goes the ball and over the net. Nobody ever instructed you how to do this. You do it by instinct. Yet if you kept the face of the bat straight and tried to get it over the net with a kind of scooping motion, it would go into the net every time. So, if you try to hit a golf ball up into the air by some means of your own, it will assuredly go along the ground. If you try to hit it forwards *along the ground*, the loft of the club will cause it to go into the air.

Perhaps I may pursue this point with an analogy from another game. I am afraid it will appeal more to the male reader, but never mind. You can save yourself hours of wasted time and can avoid, in the graphic phrase of that greatest of all women golfers, the late Mrs. "Babe" Zaharias, "getting fouled up in the mechanics of the game", if you imagine the golf shot to be the same as hitting a half-volley at cricket *straight back to the bowler and without giving a catch.*

If you think of this, you won't heave round to the left, all right shoulder, as so many golfers do—thus coming across the ball and slicing it away in a curve to the right—because this shot would not have gone straight back to the bowler. It would have started towards mid-on and curved away to mid-off. Similarly, you won't lean back on the right foot and try to scoop the ball up into the air because in that way you would almost certainly be giving a catch.

So concentrate on hitting it *forwards* and the club will assure that it goes in the air. How high in the air depends not on you but solely on the loft on the face of the club.

Most beginners, if asked to name the two most important fingers in playing golf, would probably name the first two on the right hand—the ones that "feel" most of the strength you put into a shot. They could not be more wrong. The two most important fingers to the beginner, and indeed to all golfers, are the last two fingers of the left hand. If they "go", everything goes.

Your right arm is by natural development stronger than your left. Furthermore, it is playing a forehand stroke, whereas your left is playing a backhand. Everything conspires to make the right overpower the left and it is worth quite a little trouble, if you become keen on golf, to strengthen your left arm and particularly the last two fingers of your left hand. Henry Cotton, incomparably the greatest British golfer since the first World War, spent years doing it. Swinging a club with your left hand alone will work wonders, and incidentally will produce in your early golfing days a better looking swing than you at first achieve with two hands. Squeezing a squash ball or even a rolled up handkerchief carried in the pocket will strengthen the fingers of your left hand and has the added advantage that nobody knows you are doing it!

Another of Cotton's "tricks", even when talking to other people, was to place the back of the left hand casually against the wall and then, without any change of expression, to press the arm as hard as possible against the wall. The only trouble is that, when you stop, after a minute or two's hard pressure, your left arm tends to rise away from your body and people ask you what on earth you are doing.

I once asked the late Archie Compston, in my opinion one of

the really great teachers of golf if you did not mind his rugged
manner, what he thought was the commonest fault of the average golfer. He replied instantly "A dummy left side." What
he meant was this. As your strong right arm bashes at the ball,
any number of things on the left side may "give", thus wasting
the force and collapsing the swing. Your left shoulder may, so
to speak, be knocked away; your left elbow may give way, or
your left wrist, or more likely the last two fingers of your left
hand. Don't let this appear too technical. It is simply within
the course of nature, especially for the beginner, that your
right side is stronger than your left. Once this is appreciated,
you can set about building up the necessary "resistance movement" on the weaker side. The sooner the better.

The oldest adage in golf is "Keep your eye on the ball."
The truth is that a good player does not really need to. John
Jacobs has an excellent "turn" in his demonstrations—or
clinics, as they are called—in which he will look someone full
in the eye and at the same time hit a perfect shot without
looking anywhere near the ball. Nevertheless, for the beginner,
"eye on the ball" it must be. You might not think there to be
anything much in this. There is nothing else to look at, so why
not look at the ball? You will be surprised. You start by gazing
fixedly at the ball. You take a swing at it—and half way down
the downswing the ball vanishes from sight. Where, then,
were you looking? Heaven knows—but not at the ball. Try it
again.

The real thing, though, is to *keep your head still*. If you look
at "strip" pictures of first class players taken from film se-
quences, you can note the position of the top of their head
against the background—trees, maybe, or a bush or a house—
and you will find that they can hit an absolutely full shot, 300
yards perhaps, without their heads moving an inch, backwards

or forwards, until the ball is safely on its way. In the case of a few it does move an inch or two, in which case it will actually move backward rather than forward as they hit the ball. Nine out of ten golfers, the writer included, tend to move their head forward with the shot, to "go with it" instead of staying behind it—thus dissipating much of the force of the blow. All I can say to the beginner is, "Start as you mean to go on." Never mind about eye on the ball. *Keep your head still.*

xiii. Putting — a "game within a game"

LIKE keeping goal at soccer, putting is a "game within a game". Plenty of people learn to hit a golf ball really well without ever learning to be good putters. Others never learn to hit the ball really well but become demon putters. The Palmers and Nicklauses of this world become millionaires because they are among the very, very few who contrive to be supremely good at both. I sometimes think that successful putting is almost a "state of mind", for the action required to knock a little ball a few feet along a specially smooth piece of grass is absurdly simple.

Weird, wonderful and uncountable are the weapons, stances,

79

methods and "secrets" by which men of otherwise reasonable intelligence have tried to master this elementary act. My only object here being to save you time in reaching sufficient proficiency to derive real pleasure from golf, I will pass on some "secrets"—they really *are* simple—which I extracted from one who in his prime may well have been the greatest putter of all time, namely, Bobby Locke.

The fact is that a putt, whether of three feet or thirty, is still a golf shot—and it has got to be a good one. A half-hit drive will still go somewhere and may or may not lose you a stroke. A mis-hit putt, from holing-out distance at any rate, is a final failure and does lose you a stroke. The first thing, therefore, whatever your method or your club, is to *make a good shot*.

This is not difficult, once you forget about the hole and the result and concentrate only on hitting the ball well. Locke reckons to hit the ball and only the ball—none of this "club lightly brushing the turf" that we read about. He hits it, to revert once again to table tennis, just as you would flip a stationary ball with your finger nail—taking aim at the exact back-centre and hitting it clean. This makes quite a noticeable high-pitched sort of "ping", whereas the not-quite-hit ones make a duller sort of "pung". The difference in sound, when he demonstrates it, is quite astonishing. Anyone who has played, or even watched, cricket or tennis will know that at these games too a well hit shot sounds quite different from a bad one.

A good way to get the point of all this is to put down four balls in a row. Hit one of them—any distance you like—and then, without looking up, try to hit the other three at exactly the same strength. The four balls should end up roughly in a row—but they won't. You will probably find that one has gone little more than two-thirds of the way. Though you hit *at* it with the same strength, you did not connect properly. Most "three-putts" come from bad distance rather than bad direction—but you cannot begin to judge distance till you know that you are going to hit the ball as you mean to. So Locke's first rule of putting is "Hit the ball cleanly, the same way every time."

His second rule re-states in simple terms an elementary principle which everybody must know but practically no golfer, in my own experience, ever thinks out for himself. It is that every putt, *so far as the striker is concerned*, is dead straight. The ground may slope—and indeed it generally does—and the ball will run in some sort of curve, especially towards the end, but this is due to the ground, not the golfer. Once you realise this, and that you are never going to be faced with a "nasty curly putt" again, it simplifies the whole business wonderfully. All you have to do—and this can only come from experience—is to decide on the degree of "borrow", aim off to allow for it, and then hit a dead straight putt at the point you have decided on. The slope will do the rest.

A fair, though not exact, comparison is rifle shooting, of which I used to do a good deal. You know perfectly well that the bullet in fact goes in an up-and-down curve, due to gravity, and if there is a wind you may adjust your sights to "lay off" for that as well. Having done all this, you direct your eye and the rifle straight at the target. All you can do is to make a good shot. What happens to the bullet, or the golf ball, when you have "fired", is beyond your control. All that you can do must be done at "this" end. The only difference between the two "shots" is that in shooting you adjust the sights, in golf you adjust your aim.

Finally Locke had a secret which everyone can copy, and means to copy, and never does. Whenever he made a putt—indeed, whenever he made any kind of shot — he went through the same "drill". It never by any chance varied. On the green his drill was to take two practice swings, of the same length and strength that he intended for the putt itself: then a pace forward to the ball: one look at the hole—and away she goes. Locke was known in Britain as a very slow player and in championships he finished nearly every round with a gap of two or three holes between him and the people in front. When he had reached his ball, however, and had surveyed the stroke to be played, taking into consideration the distance, the slope, the wind, the day of the month, the state of the tide and, I dare say, several other things as well, he was then in fact a quick player. Once his mind was made up, he put the drill into action, set the machine in motion and away went the ball.

I remember watching him win his first open championship at Sandwich. In the last round disaster overtook him at the 16th hole and he took three dreadful putts. When all seemed lost, he put a wonderful second shot within 10 feet of the 17th and holed the putt for a 3. So now here he was, on the 18th, with just this one 4-foot putt to tie with Harry Bradshaw. This is a situation in which almost every golfer has at some time imagined himself. The huge crowd, the dead silence, and "This to tie for the Open." Surely, I thought, he must take one extra look at the hole for this one? But no. The drill saw him through. Two practice swings, pace forward, and away it went. Right in to the middle.

Of course, I do not suggest that we ought all to copy Locke. Some people may care to take a longer time, some even less, but one of the most certain causes of bad play—bad, that is, judged by our own personal standard, however low it may be —is "thinking" while playing the shot instead of thinking first and then, for better or for worse, stepping up to the ball and hitting it. A set "drill" is a wonderful aid to getting our very imperfect machine in motion.

xiv. Who governs golf?

You can enjoy playing golf without having the remotest idea
as to who makes the Rules under which the game is played
or who runs the championships which you read about or watch
on the television. Nevertheless, golf is not merely a business of
knocking a little ball along with a stick. It has an "atmosphere"
of its own and I cannot help feeling that the newcomer may
derive a good deal more pleasure from the game and a greater
sense of "belonging", if he knows, roughly speaking, who does
what in the background. The reader need have no fear, however, that I propose to embark on a long and detailed treatise
on the various ruling bodies in golf.

The supreme authority is, of course, the Royal and Ancient Golf Club of St. Andrews, and a remarkable institution it is. It was founded in 1754 and was known as the St. Andrews Golf Club till His Majesty King William IV bestowed its present title in 1834. The grey stone clubhouse, which presides as a background to the stage on which so many golfing dramas have been played, was built in 1840.

The R. and A., though it elects its own members, is in fact, in the fashionable word of the day, a most "democratic" body. There are now about 1,000 members, with several hundred "supernumerary" members in distant parts of the world, and these include men who are, or have been, distinguished in almost every walk of life, together with an up-and-coming younger element likely to play a useful part in the government of the game later on.

The Club has various Committees, of which the best known are the Championship and the Rules of Golf. The Championship Committee runs the Open, Amateur, Youths' and Boys' Championships and, considering that it is a voluntary body, undertakes a very considerable financial responsibility. The Open, for instance, is entirely self-supporting and with a prize list of £40,000 and running costs of perhaps £20,000 is no mean promotion. Though a dozen commercial sponsors could be found to take it on only too gladly, the R. and A. feel that it should at all costs remain independent. Apart from a few hundred pounds in television rights, the only source of revenue is gate money. This is why it can only profitably be played in areas with a keen golfing population and on courses where not too large a proportion can get in without paying. It is also the main reason why in 1966 it was decided to extend it to four days instead of three, with the final round on a Saturday.

The members of the R. and A. hold two Business Meetings a year, coinciding with competitions for the Spring and

utumn Medals. In numbers which seem to increase every
ear they assemble in the Big Room overlooking the first tee;
e blinds are drawn over the tall windows against the setting
n; the chairmen of the various Committees read out their
ports and submit to questions; and the meeting is often
er in twenty minutes. This, however, is the Parliament of
olf, one man one vote, and it is this body which is the
entual arbiter of questions which in the end affect every
lfer. The Rules of Golf Committee, for instance, may make
commendations. They will become Rules only when the
usiness Meeting agrees.

The Captain is chosen each year by secret consultation
tween all the living past Captains—and an invariably well-
pt secret it is—and on Medal Day in September he is
corted out to the first tee by those past Captains who are
esent and, as the clock strikes 8 a.m., he "drives himself
to office". His ball is solemnly tee-ed up by the Club's
norary professional; the ancient cannon is lined up beside
e tee; and the caddies assemble at strategic positions on the
irway, the one fortunate enough to retrieve the ball being
warded with a golden sovereign. This is a stroke for which he
s been preparing for six months, and it is no mean ordeal.
e knows that the cannon, only a few feet away, is going to
off with a roar which will reverberate through the ancient
wn, and he can see what the caddies think of him by where
ey stand. When the then Prince of Wales, later King Edward
III, drove himself in in 1922, Sir Guy Campbell wrote in
he Times that some of the caddies stood "disloyally close to
e tee"—and, as it proved, they were right!

Every year since 1754 the Captain has appended a silver
ll to the Silver Club (the third club, now) but the Royal
iptains, the two Princes of Wales (Edward VII and Edward
III) 1863 and 1922; the Duke of York (George VI) 1930;

85

and the Duke of Kent, 1937; have each appended a gold ba
These three silver clubs, festooned with gold and silver ball
are outstanding among the spectacular Trophies and Regal
of the Club which are admired by hundreds of visitors eve
year.

The R. and A. also takes care of the Walker Cup matc
against the United States every two years, though nowada
it delegates a good deal of the team selection to representativ
of the National Unions, and it manages the teams selected f
the Eisenhower Trophy (every four years for teams of fo
from all over the world) and the Commonwealth tourname
(every five years, also for teams of four).

The National Unions

Each of the four countries has a national Golf Union, Ei
and Northern Ireland for this purpose counting as one ar
known as the Golfing Union of Ireland, a fact which may l
regarded as no small tribute to the unifying genius of go
The four Unions together also have a "Union" of their ow
known as the Council of National Golf Unions or C.O.N.G.U
These Unions play a useful part in golf. Each of them conduc
a national championship, indeed the English Golf Union ru
two—the match play championship, which was begun in 192
and the competition for the Brabazon Trophy, which in 19
was deemed to be the stroke play championship.

The Unions also run the annual four-cornered internation
matches, in each country in turn, each country playing t
other three, ten a side, foursomes in the morning, singles
the afternoon; and here perhaps is amateur golf at its ve
best. The main function of the Unions, however, ever since
was delegated to them by the R. and A. in 1924, has been
devise, and then from time to time revise, a method of fixir

cratch scores for courses as a basis for a general system of
andicapping, and this, in an imperfect world, they have done
ith much hard work and as much success as could be hoped.
have said something of this system in the chapter on Handi-
aps.

Nearly every County has a Union of its own, though some-
mes a number of smaller ones—"smaller", that is, from
ne golfing point of view—combine together, as with Lei-
estershire and Rutland, and Berks, Bucks and Oxon. These
Unions each run a County Championship of their own and
lay County matches against each other, and each year the
hampions of all the Counties assemble for a day's golf to
stablish a "champion of champions".

County golf engenders tremendous enthusiasm, especially
a parts more distant from the vast, sprawling mass of the
netropolis, where the golfer may be excused for not being
articularly conscious of what County he is in. Younger readers
f this book, when they have passed the stage of playing in
unior competitions (of which to my mind there are not nearly
nough, considering how often courses are free in mid-week
uring school holidays) should set their sights at their County
eam and County championship. Here they will experience
ll the stresses and strains, the disasters, disappointments and
erhaps even triumphs that are endured by the great cham-
ions of golf. The latter may miss a putt to win the Open.
hey won't *feel* it any more acutely than the younger golfer
ho misses it to win his first County championship.

The Professional Golfers Association

The P.G.A. was formed in 1901, in the heyday of the
Great Triumvirate—Harry Vardon, J. H. Taylor and James
Braid. Such men were immensely respected in their day. They
vere men of the greatest integrity and set a standard of be-

haviour, both on and off the course, which has influenced th
profession ever since. It was perhaps J. H. Taylor more tha
any who saw the need for some sort of Association whic
would help the smaller man and generally advance the cau
of professional golf. Such an Association could encourage th
promotion of tournaments, help its members to find jobs, ru
a benevolent fund, and in all manner of ways assist membe
who by the very nature of their jobs were scattered all ove
the country.

They were aided in their early stages by Lord Riddell, wh
in 1903 started for them the "News of the World" tourna
ment, which in 1946 became recognised as the profession
match play championship. It is fair to say that professional go
owes much to the early generosity and sustained interest c
this newspaper, first through Lord Riddell, then through th
late Sir Emsley Carr and, at the present writing, his son, S
William.

Prize money for the first "News of the World" tourname
was £200—the equivalent, I suppose, of several thousa
pounds today—but nowadays the professionals regularly pl
for more than £100,000 in a single season and a clear distin
tion, though not quite so complete as in the United State
has arisen between the club professionals and the profession
players of golf. Even in this country, a few of the latter ma
reap a five-figure income. The "order of merit" as a resu
of certain specified tournaments also decides the team whi
every second year plays for the Ryder Cup against the Unite
States.

An allied but independent body is the Professional Golfe
Co-operative Association, with headquarters in Londo
Almost every club professional has an account with th
P.G.C.A., together with invaluable credit which enables hi
to keep his stock of clubs, balls, trolleys, clothing and su

88

like. This in turn is of value to the club golfer, for whom the professional can quickly obtain anything relating to the game.

Ladies Golf Union

The first lady golfer to be mentioned as such was beheaded on February 18, 1584. She was Mary Queen of Scots. As evidence of her indifference to the murder of her husband, the Earl of Darnley, it was quoted at her trial that she had been playing golf in the fields around Seton within a few days of his death. We may pass over the intervening 309 years, however, and say merely that the present Ladies Golf Union was formed by representatives of eleven clubs, called together by the Wimbledon Ladies Club in 1893. The ladies accept the Rules laid down by the Royal and Ancient but in all other respects run their own affairs.

In the 90's ladies' golf had begun to blossom forth from the days when it was held to be indecorous for a female player to raise the club above her shoulder and the ladies therefore had special little courses of their own, the longest hole being about 80 yards. More and more clubs were formed and soon they were wanting a "championship week" in which everyone, handicap players included, could gather once a year. So the first objects of the Ladies Golf Union were almost identical with that of the men's national Unions—to run a championship and to prepare some common yardstick for fixing the scratch scores of every club, so that everyone's handicap would have been fixed on the same basis.

In the latter they were at once, and have remained, more successful than the men. As I have previously quoted, many men never take out a card and pencil and count their score at all. The L.G.U., however, will have none of this. The woman golfer has got to put in a certain number of signed scorecards—or else. Regional "handicap managers" help to

89

keep the scheme in good order and it is fair to say that women golfers respond where the men would probably rebel. They are helped by the fact that they hold many mid-week meetings and thus have more opportunity of putting in the requisite number of cards. The women's handicapping system—though no better in theory—is for this reason much more effective in practice than the men's.

The L.G.U. run the Curtis Cup match, with notable success, against the United States and, until the Walker Cup team of 1965, the Curtis Cup team of 1958 were the only players, male or female, professional or amateur, to halve a match in America.

xv. And the best of luck!

WELL, there you are. I end, as I began, by saying how much I envy you if you are about to get started in golf. I have had it. You have got it all to come—including the times when the game makes you so mad that you determine to give it up. At one moment it drives you nearly to suicide; at the next you find yourself feeling that life has never been quite so good. Progress, I should warn you, comes in stages. It is rather like climbing a ladder. You gain one rung, then slip back two, then gain three and think what a clever fellow you are—this being the moment when for a certainty you slip back two again.

Never mind. Gradually you find that your highest point is a little higher than it used to be and your lowest a little less low, and now you are committed to membership of what that greatest of golf writers, Bernard Darwin, called "the bravest, stupidest race in the world, the unconvincible, inextinguishable race of golfers". If this book has done anything to help to set you on the way to enjoying your share of the good fun and good company of golf, then I shall indeed be pleased.

Where to learn:

1. From the professional at your nearest golf club.

2. At a driving range or golf course—see the Golf Course Guide or enquire at your local authority office.

3. On a course of instruction arranged by:

   a) The Central Council of Physical Recreation, 26, Park Crescent, London, W.1.

   b) Your local Education Authority.

   c) Certain holiday providing organisations, e.g. The Holiday Fellowship, 152, Great North Way, Hendon, London, N.W.4.

   d) Under the Golf Foundation Scheme (If you are a pupil at school or attending a full-time course of education at a College or University).

Useful publications:—

Some Guidance to the Rules of Golf—free from the Golf Foundation.

The Golf Course Guide by Donald Steel—published by Collins—price 75p. (Location and particulars of all golf courses in Great Britain, Ireland with green fees cost, etc.)

The Golfers Handbook—published by The Golfers Handbook, 113, St. Vincent Street, Glasgow, C.2—price £2.50.

Useful addresses:—

The Golf Foundation, City Wall House, 84–90 Chiswell Street, London, EC 1Y 4TN.

The Professional Golfers' Association, National Headquarters, The Kennington Oval, Kennington, London, S.E.11.

The English Golf Union, 12a, Denmark Street, Wokingham, Berkshire.

THE BOGEY MAN

George Plimpton

George Plimpton's brilliant and supremely amusing book about his experiences on the pro-golf circuit. Here is his account of his adventures playing as an amateur in three of the richest tournaments in America.

Just read the press comments :

"Plimpton will interest even the man who can't tell a pitching wedge from a putter . . . this is really a book about a kind of madness with rules, and anyone can appreciate the appeal of that" *Newsweek*

"Golf is a lonely game, and in Plimpton's case it is lonelier than usual. He is always at a run to catch up with other members of his four: he is a figure scuttling across the course while Palmer and his army wait and wonder. For some demented reason, he has written a deeply likeable book" *Washington Post*

"Brilliantly funny and perceptive" *The Observer*

"Humorous, but also agonizing, and unfailingly fascinating!" *The New York Times*

GET INTO THE SWING OF THINGS
WITH THE CORONET
GOLF SERIES

Tommy Armour

☐ 01044 4   HOW TO PLAY YOUR BEST GOLF
ALL THE TIME   30p

Jack Nicklaus

☐ 04348 2   THE BEST WAY TO BETTER GOLF No. 1   25p

☐ 10539 9   THE BEST WAY TO BETTER GOLF No. 2   25p

☐ 15475 6   THE BEST WAY TO BETTER GOLF No. 3   25p

George Plimpton

☐ 12616 7   THE BOGEY MAN   35p

All these books are available at your bookshop or newsagent, or can be ordered direct from the publisher. Just tick the titles you want and fill in the form below.

....

CORONET BOOKS, Cash Sales Department, Kernick Industrial Estate, Penryn, Cornwall.

Please send cheque or postal order. No currency, and allow 5p per book (4p per book on orders of five copies and over) to cover the cost of postage and packing in U.K., 5p per copy overseas.

Name..

Address..

....